Adult Coloring Book: Stress Relief and Relaxation

Original Hand-drawn Designs

Mix Books Adult Coloring

Adult Coloring Book: Stress Relief and Relaxation: Original Designs
Copyright Mix Books, LLC 2015

mix-booksonline.com

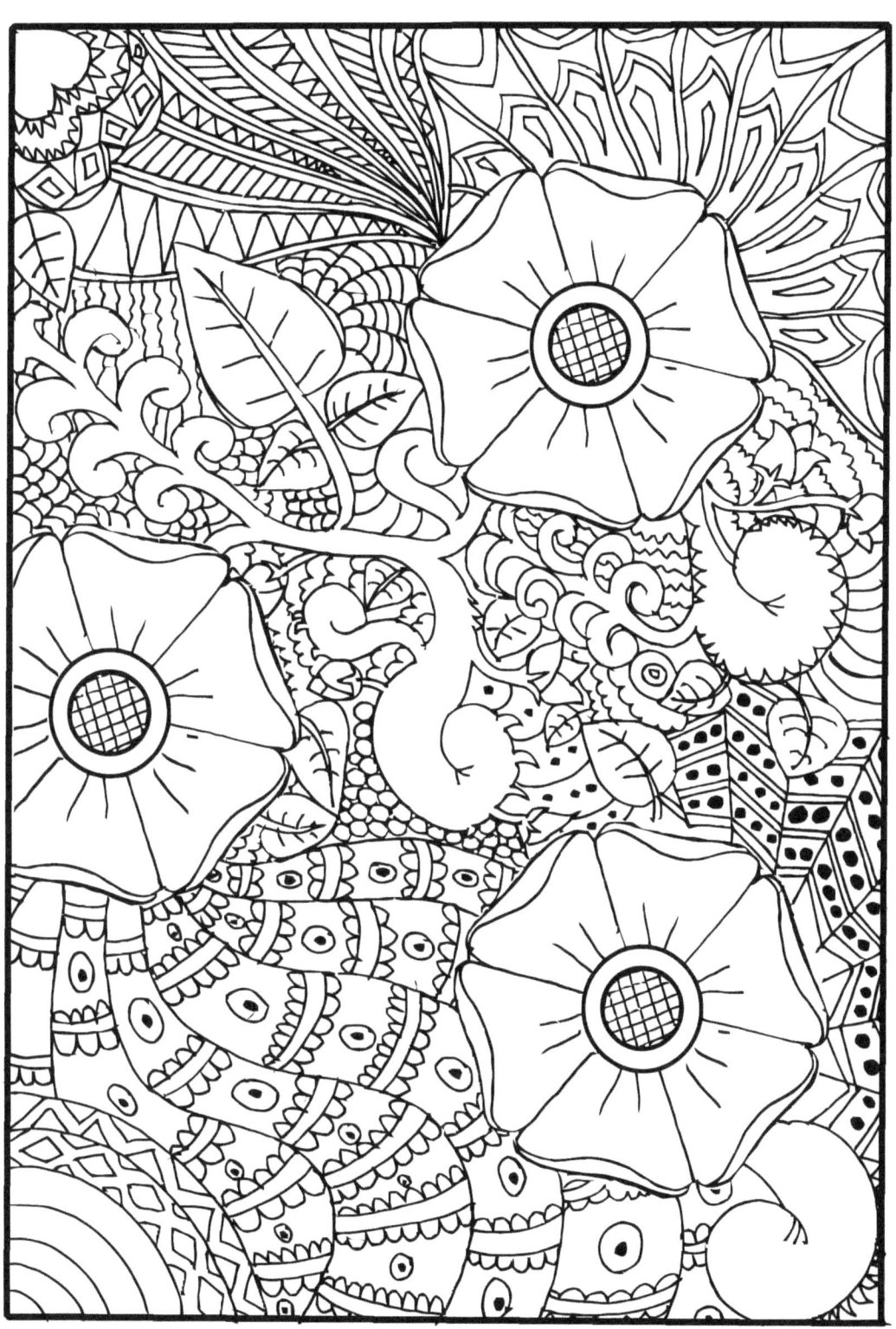

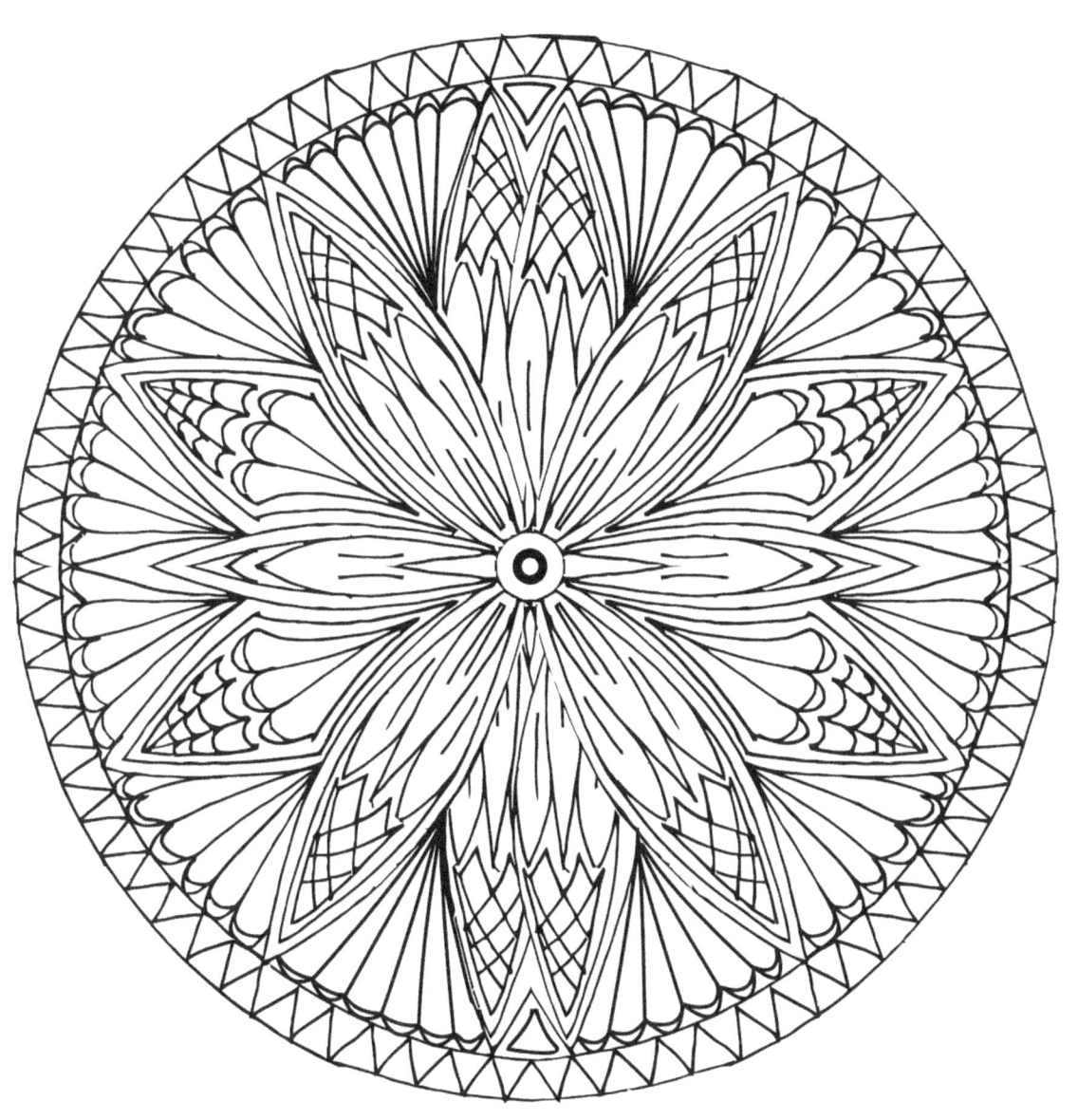

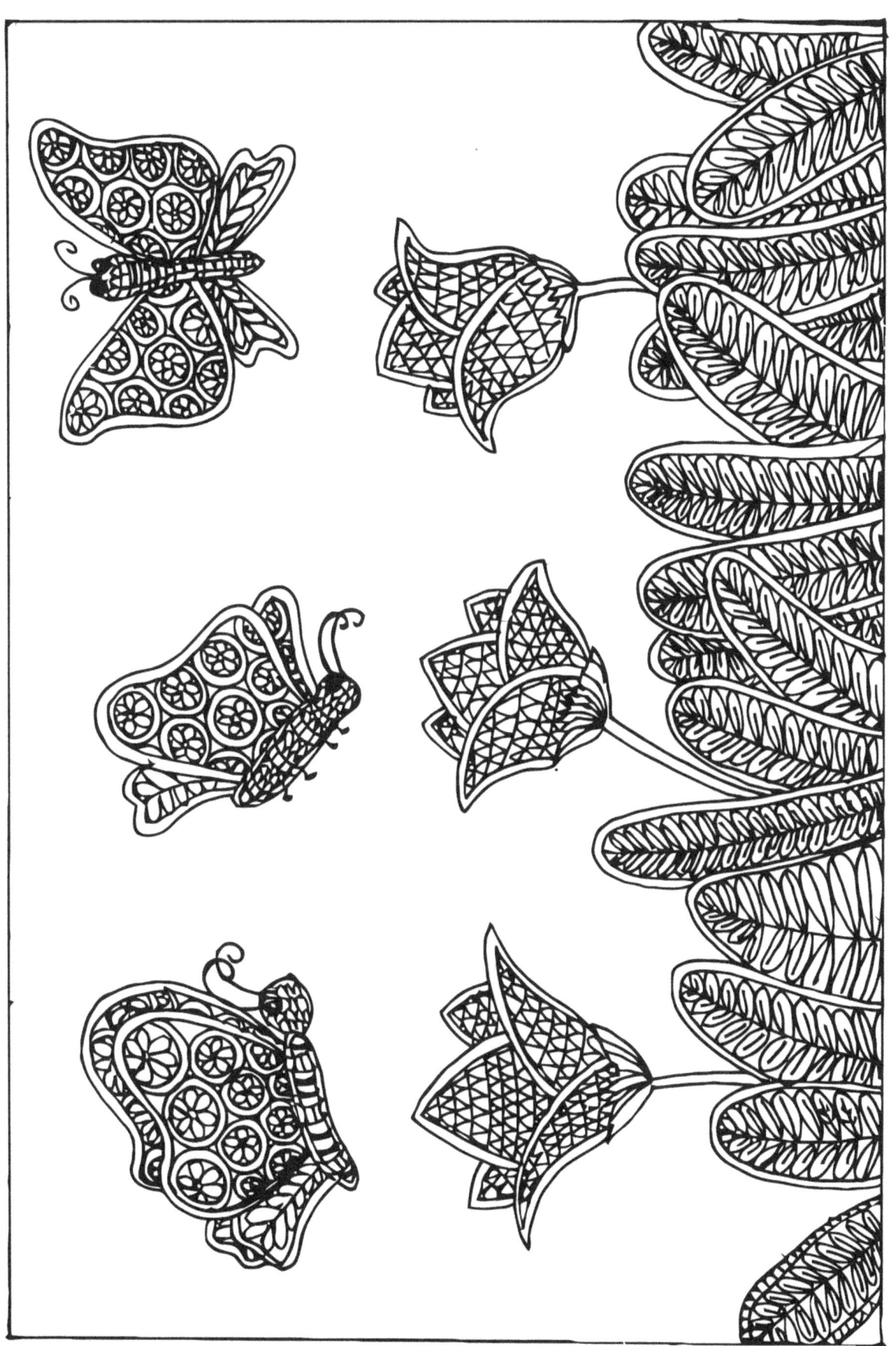

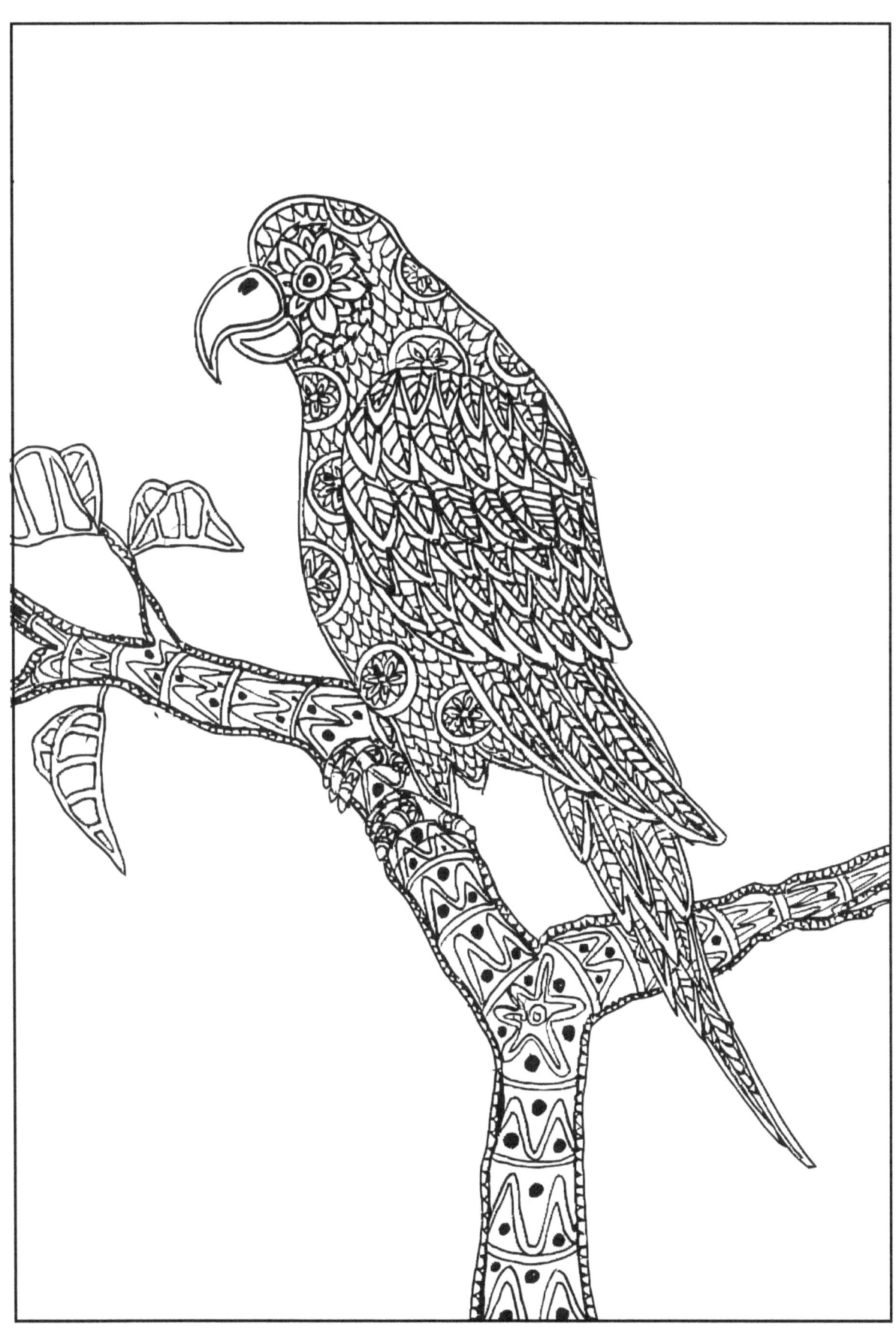

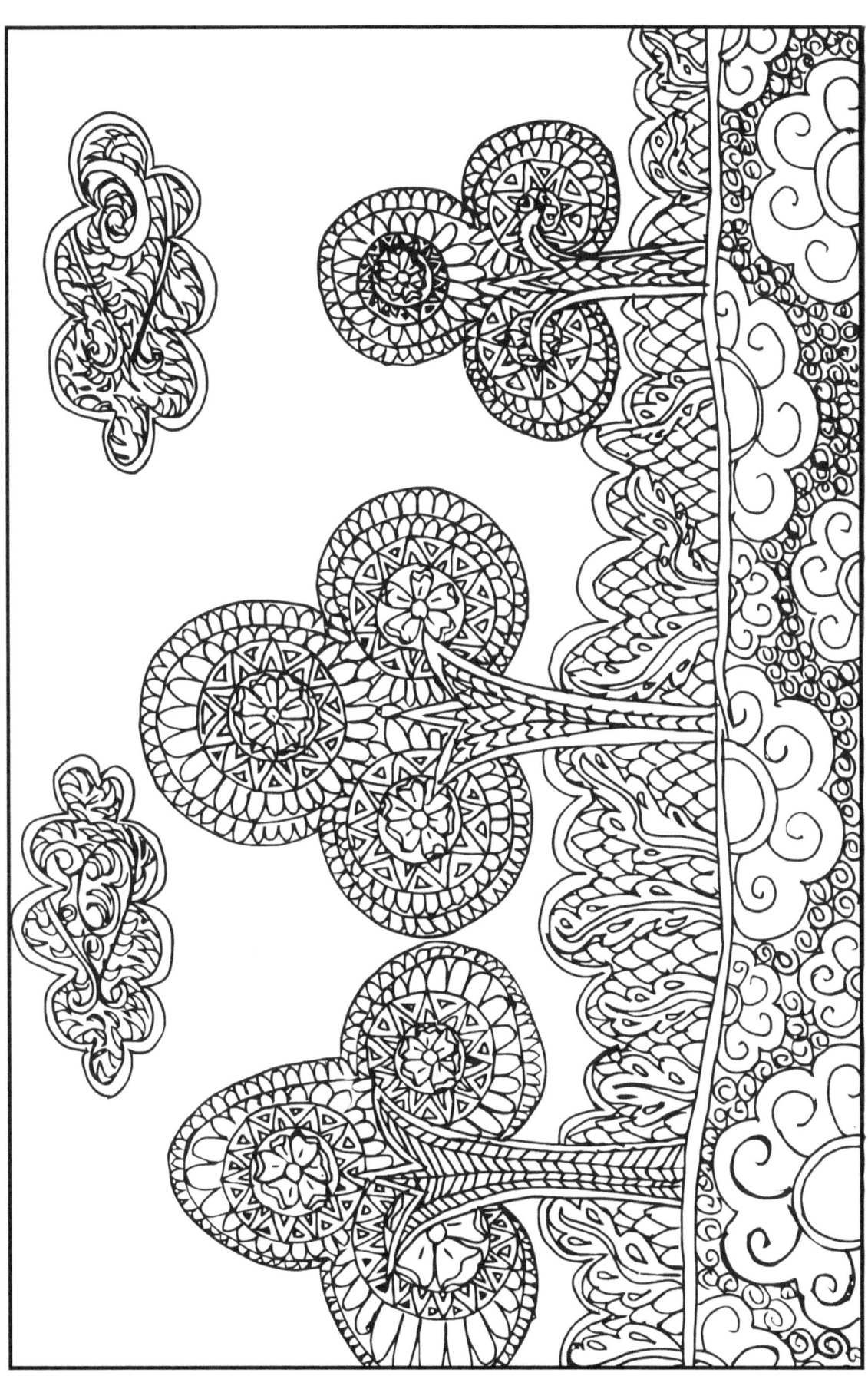

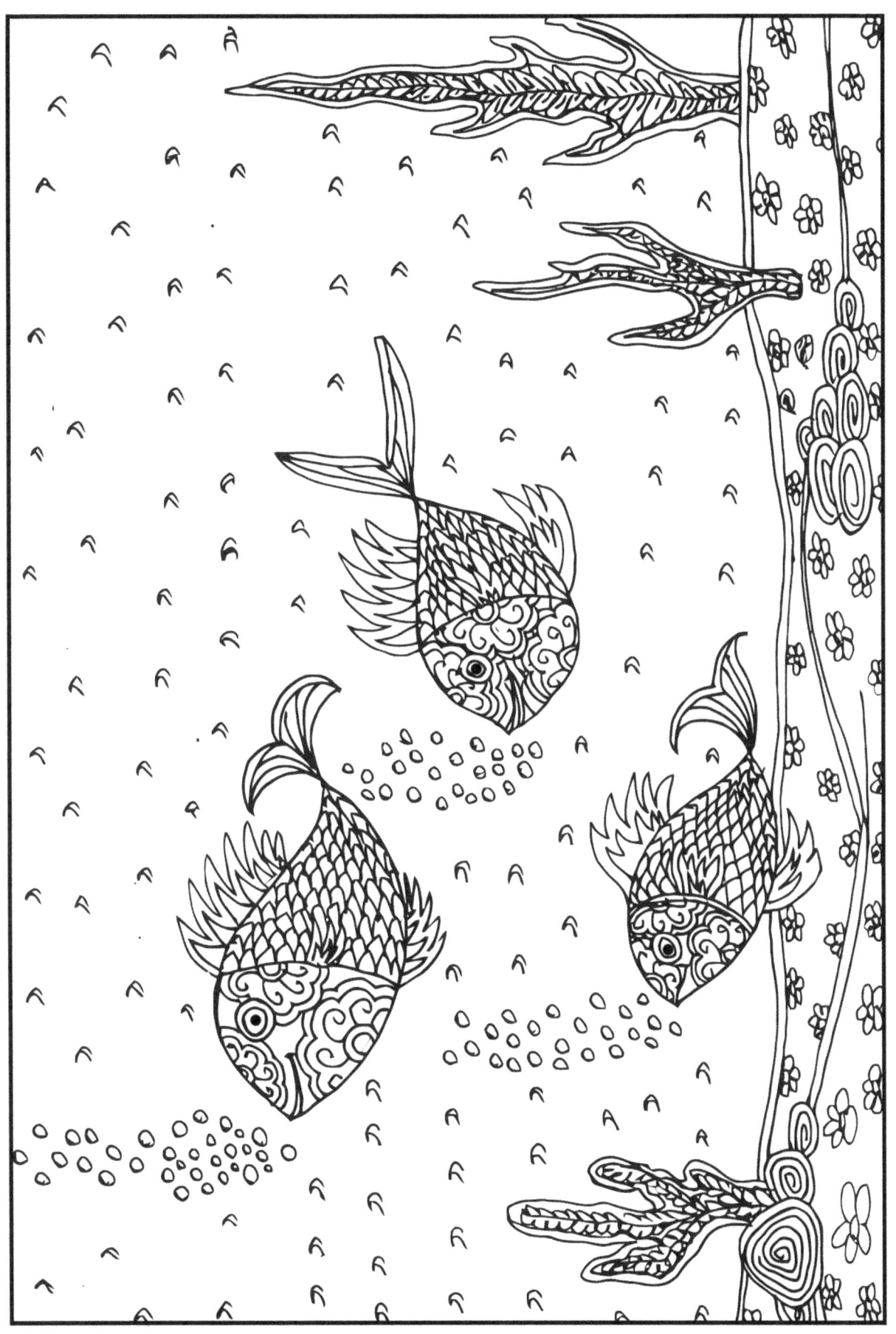

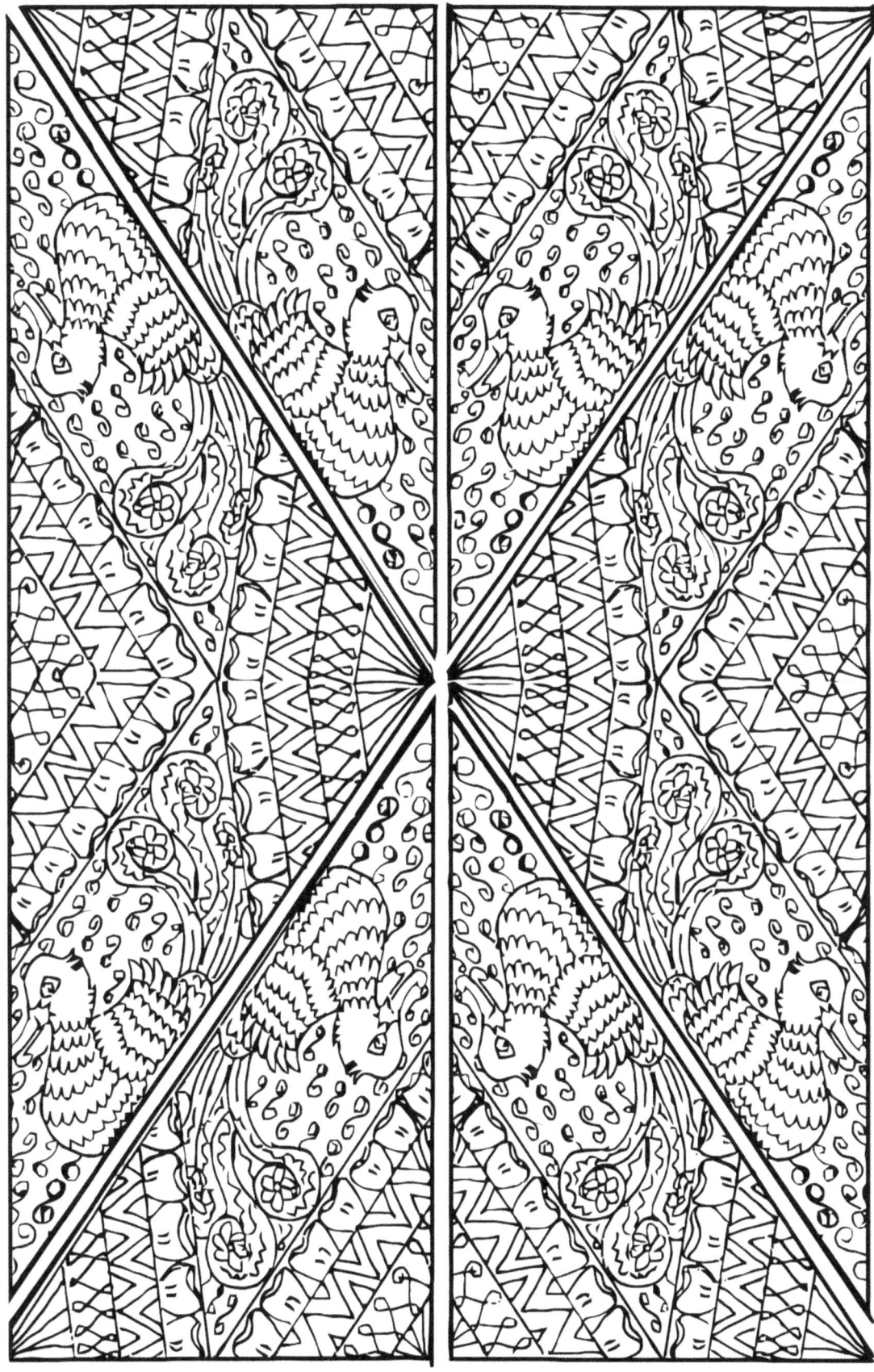

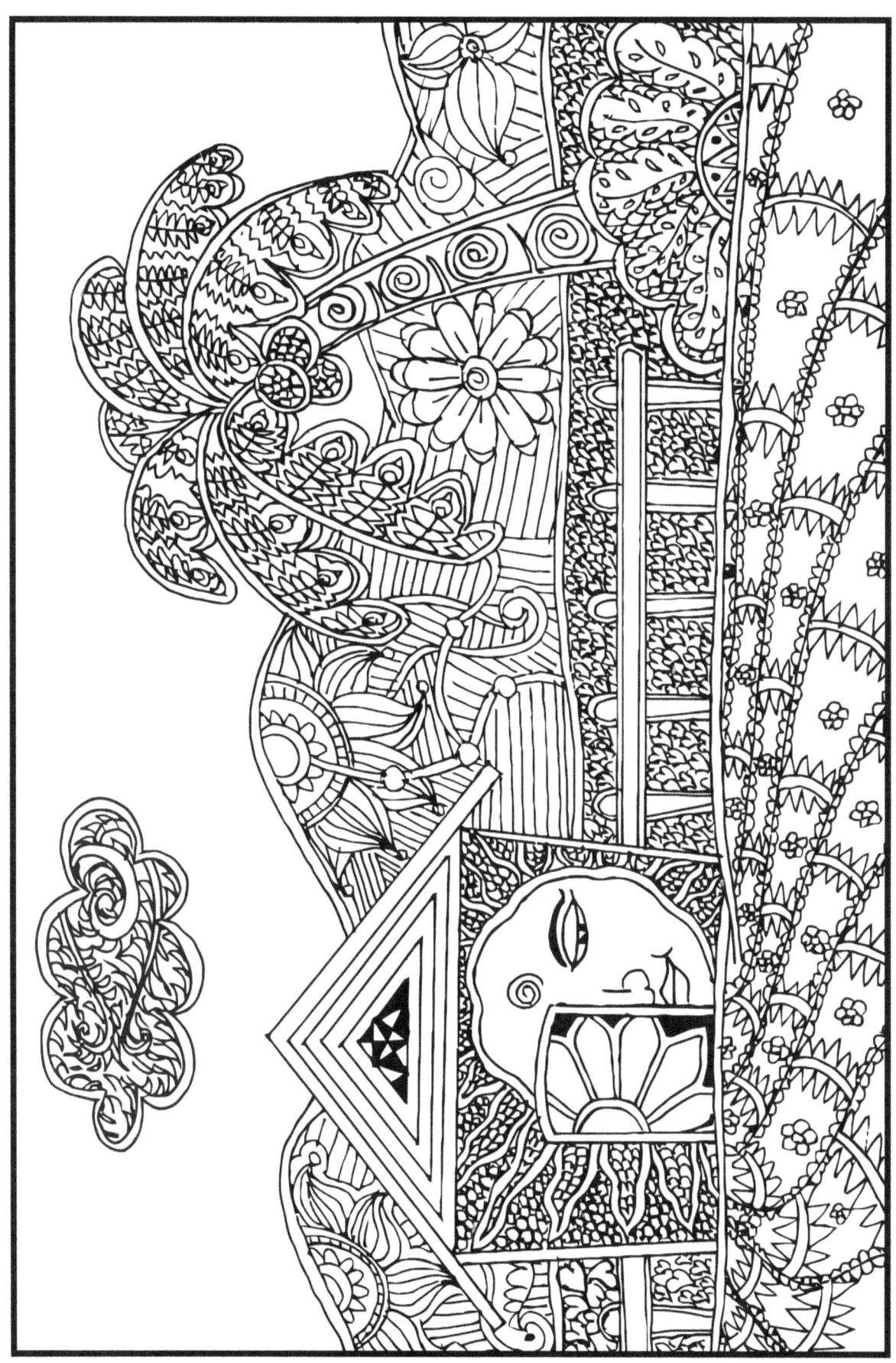

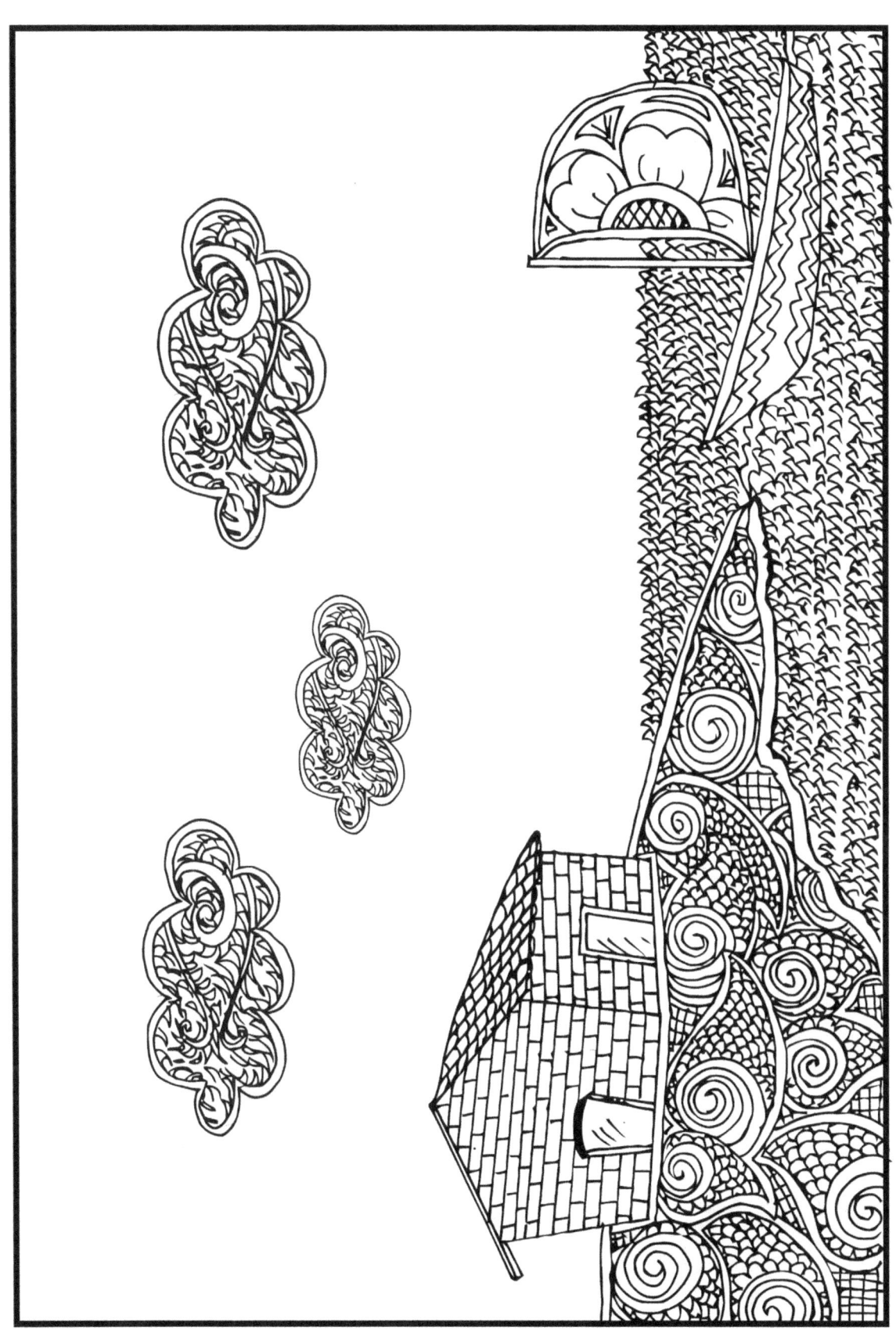

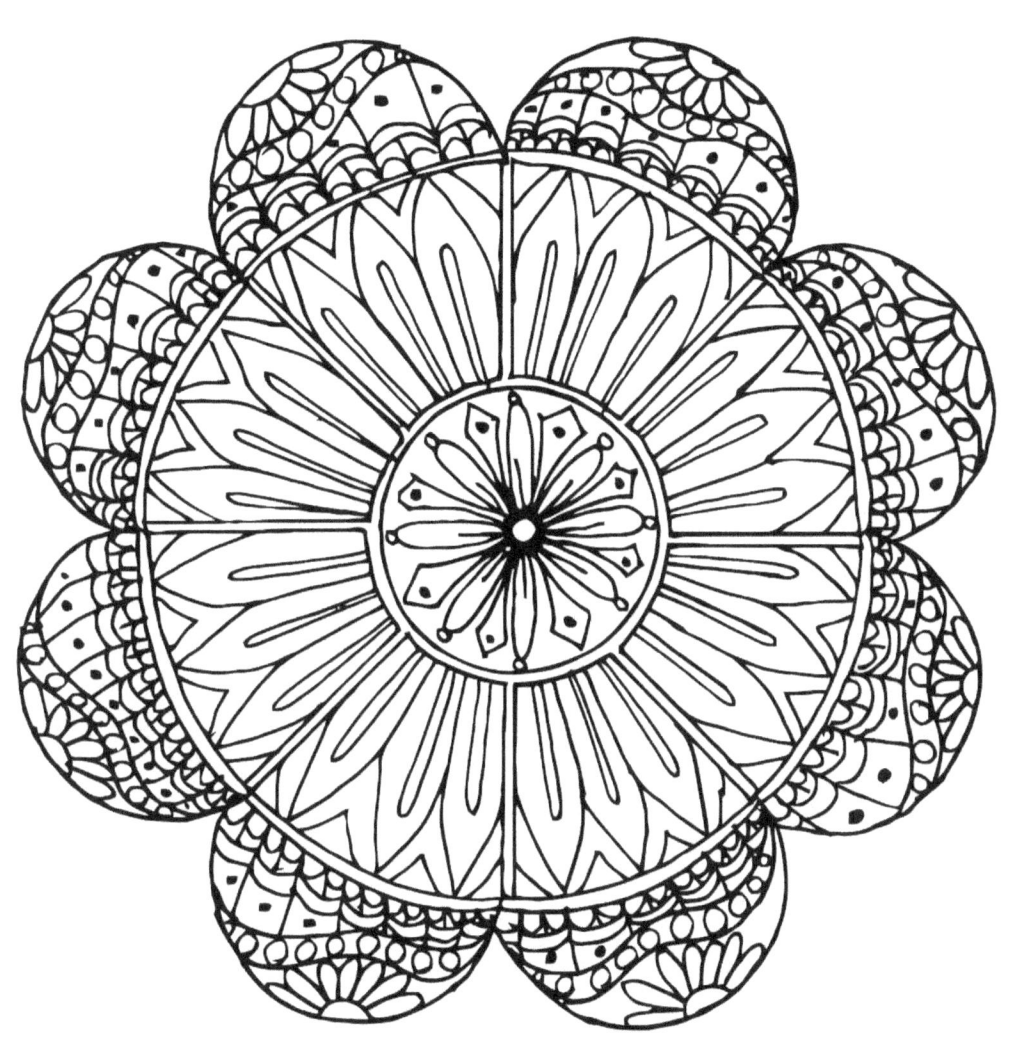

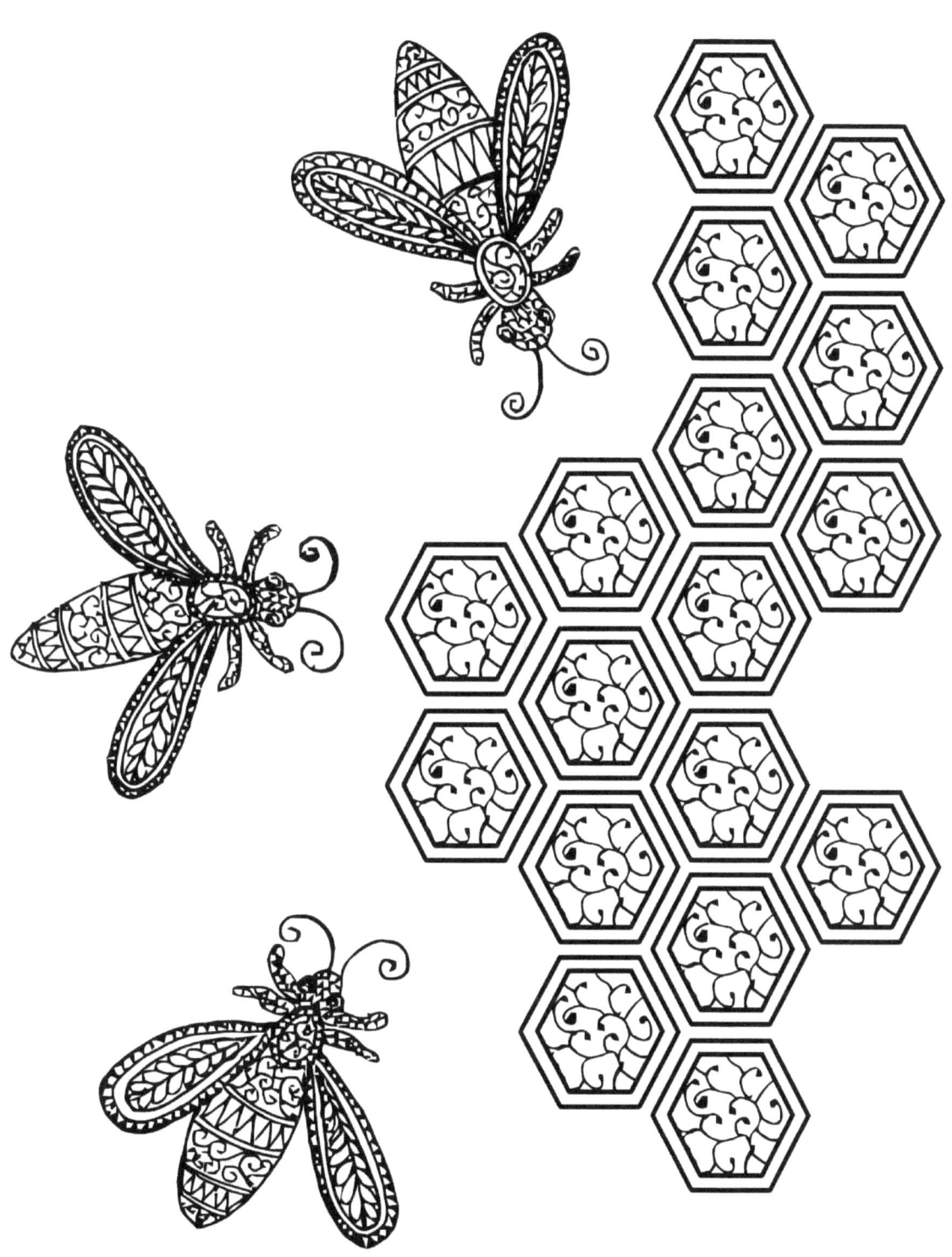

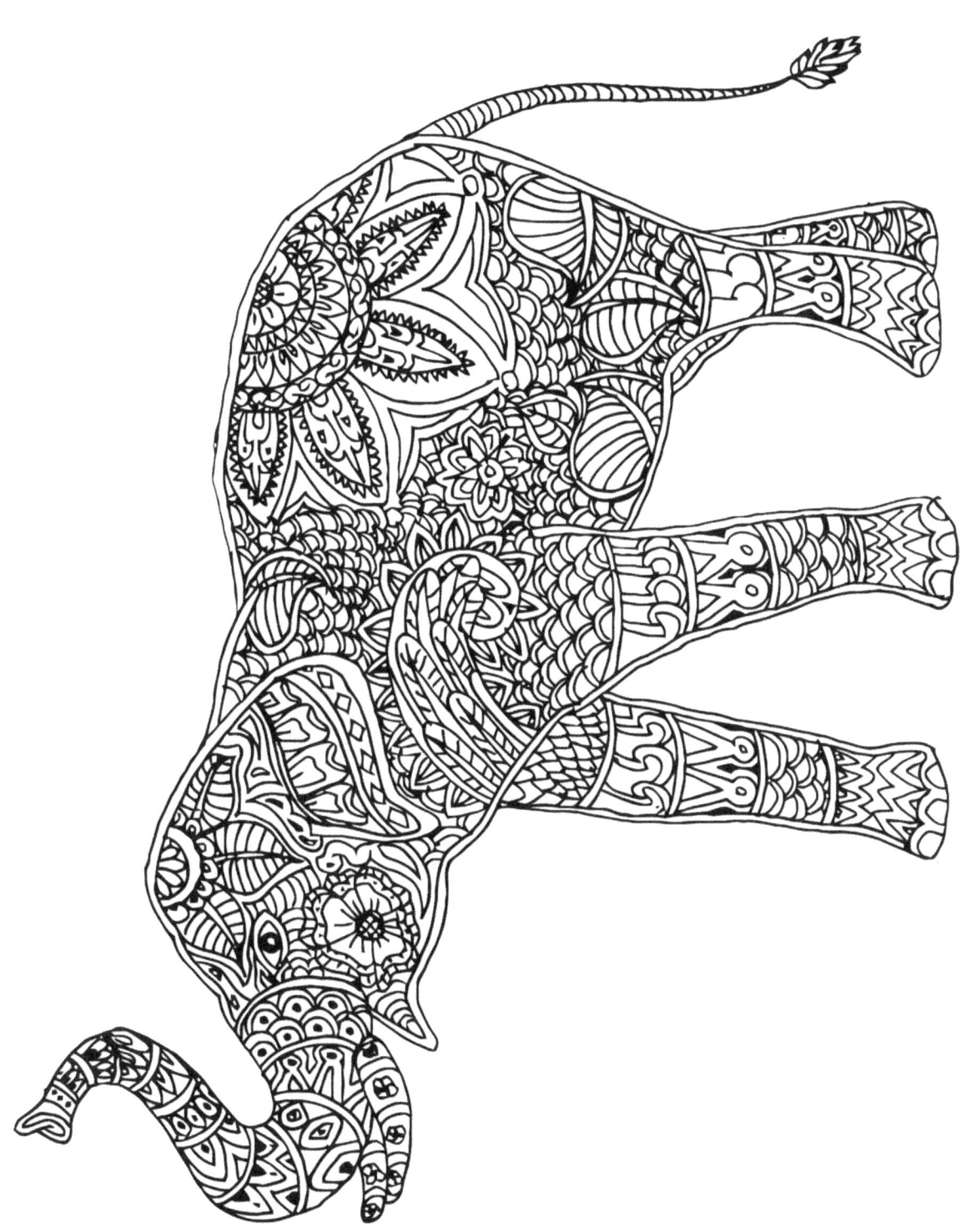

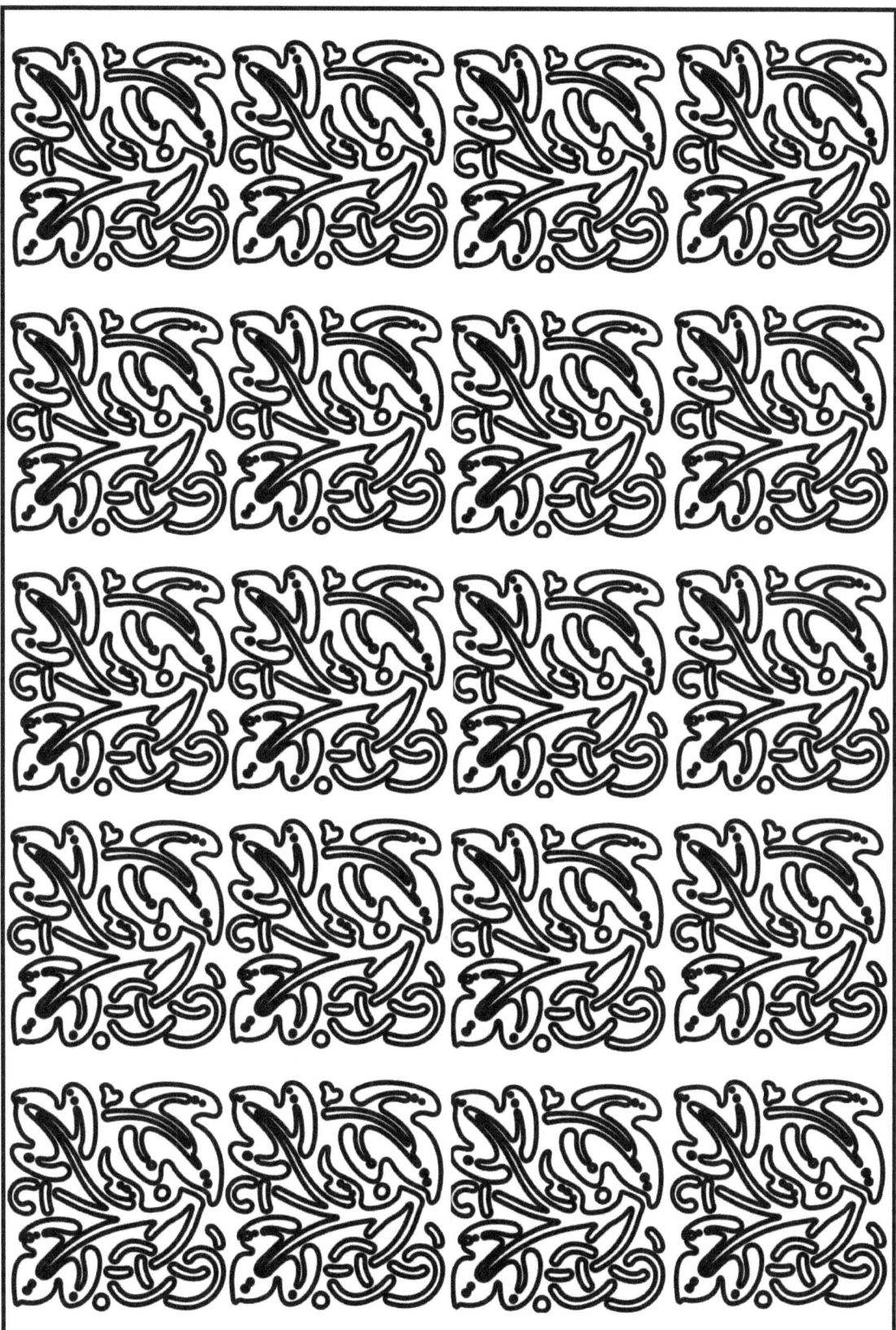

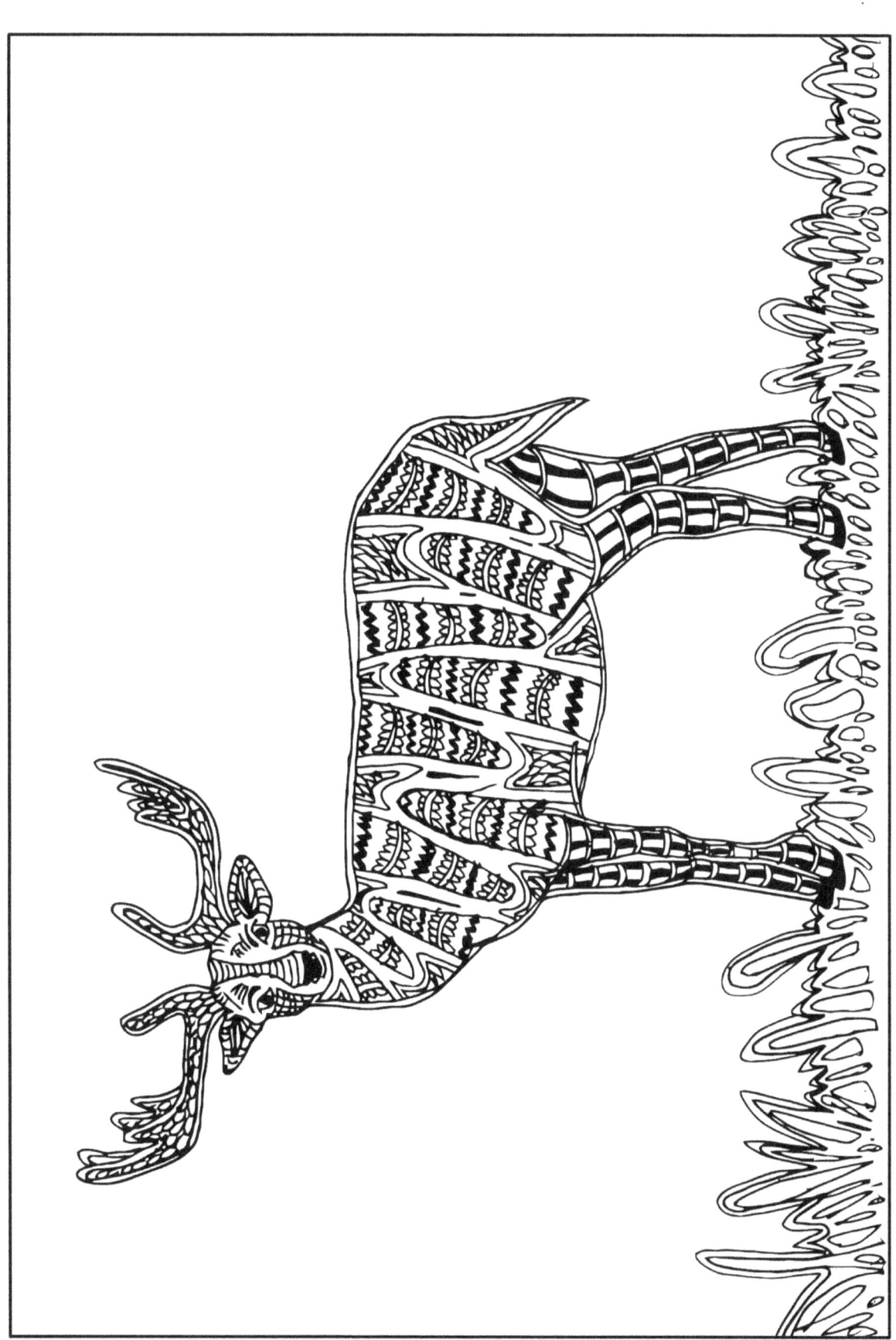

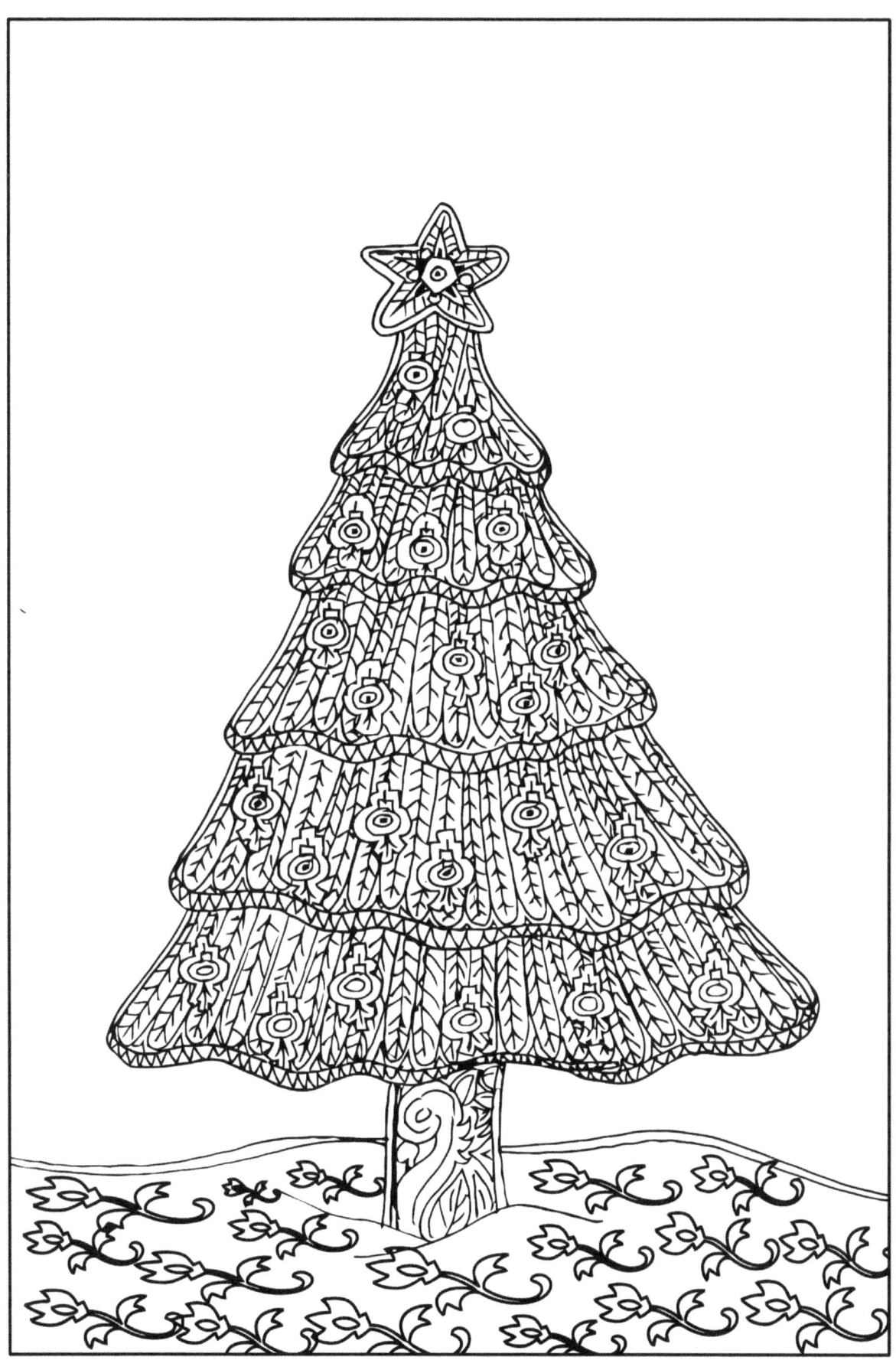

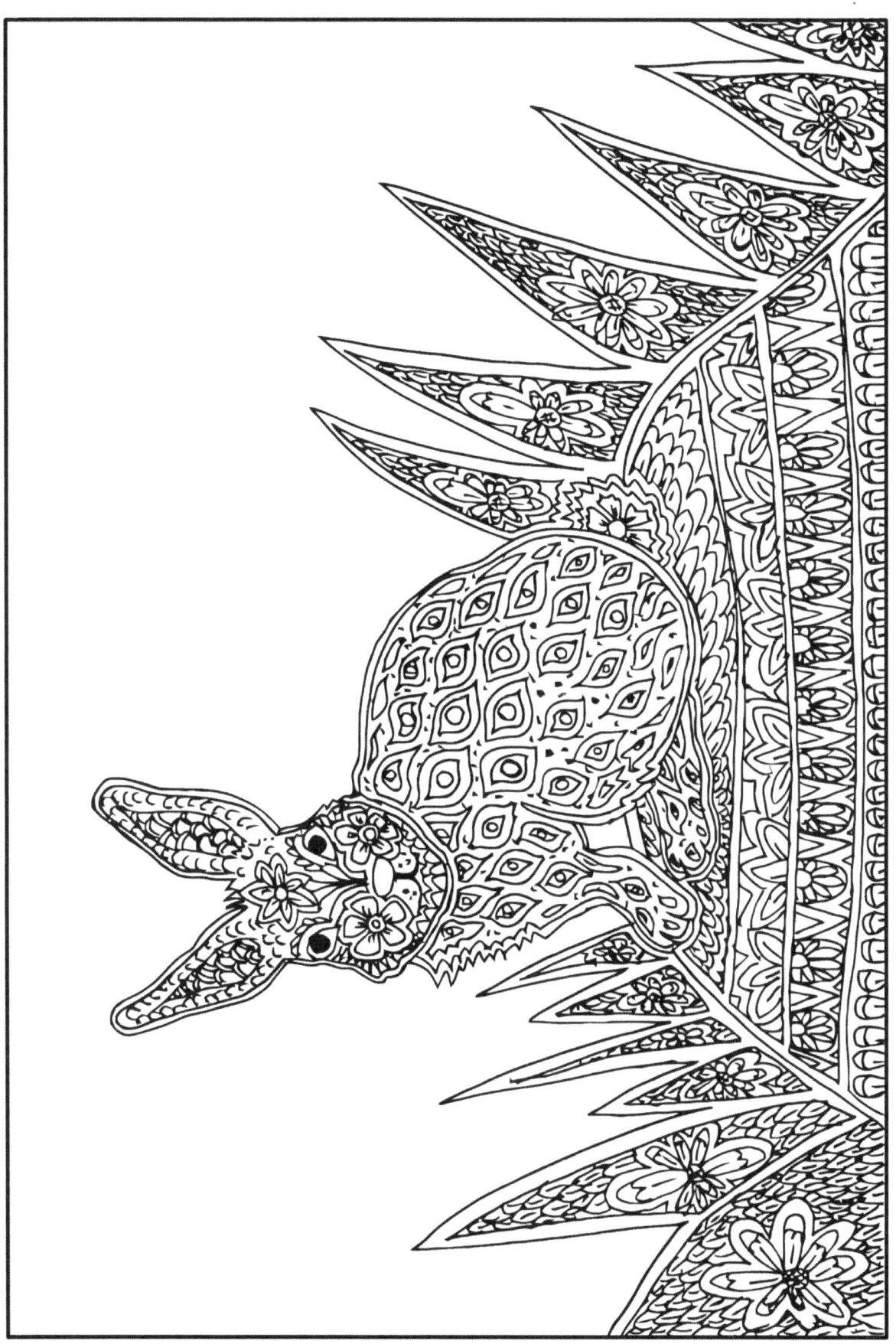

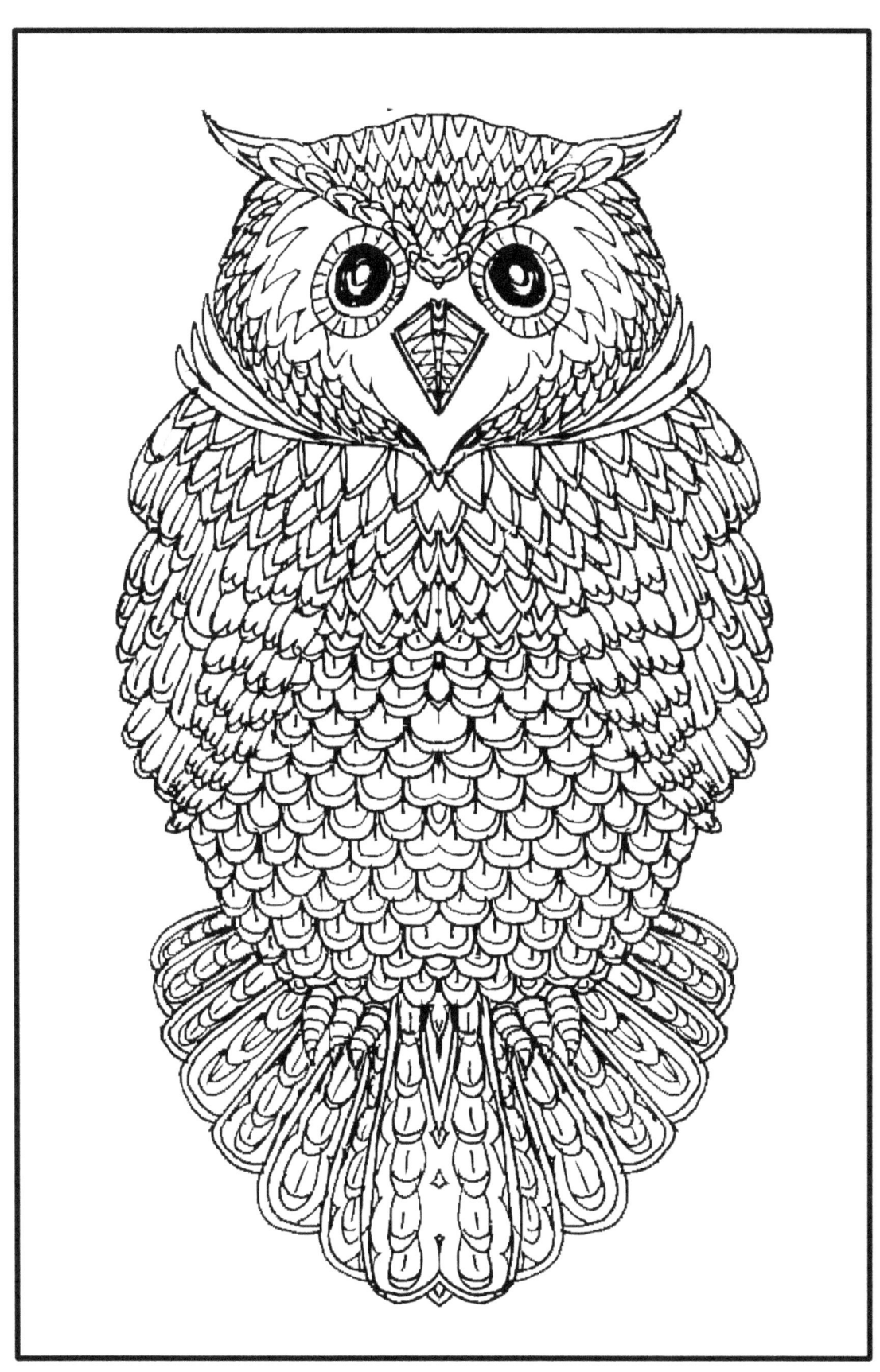

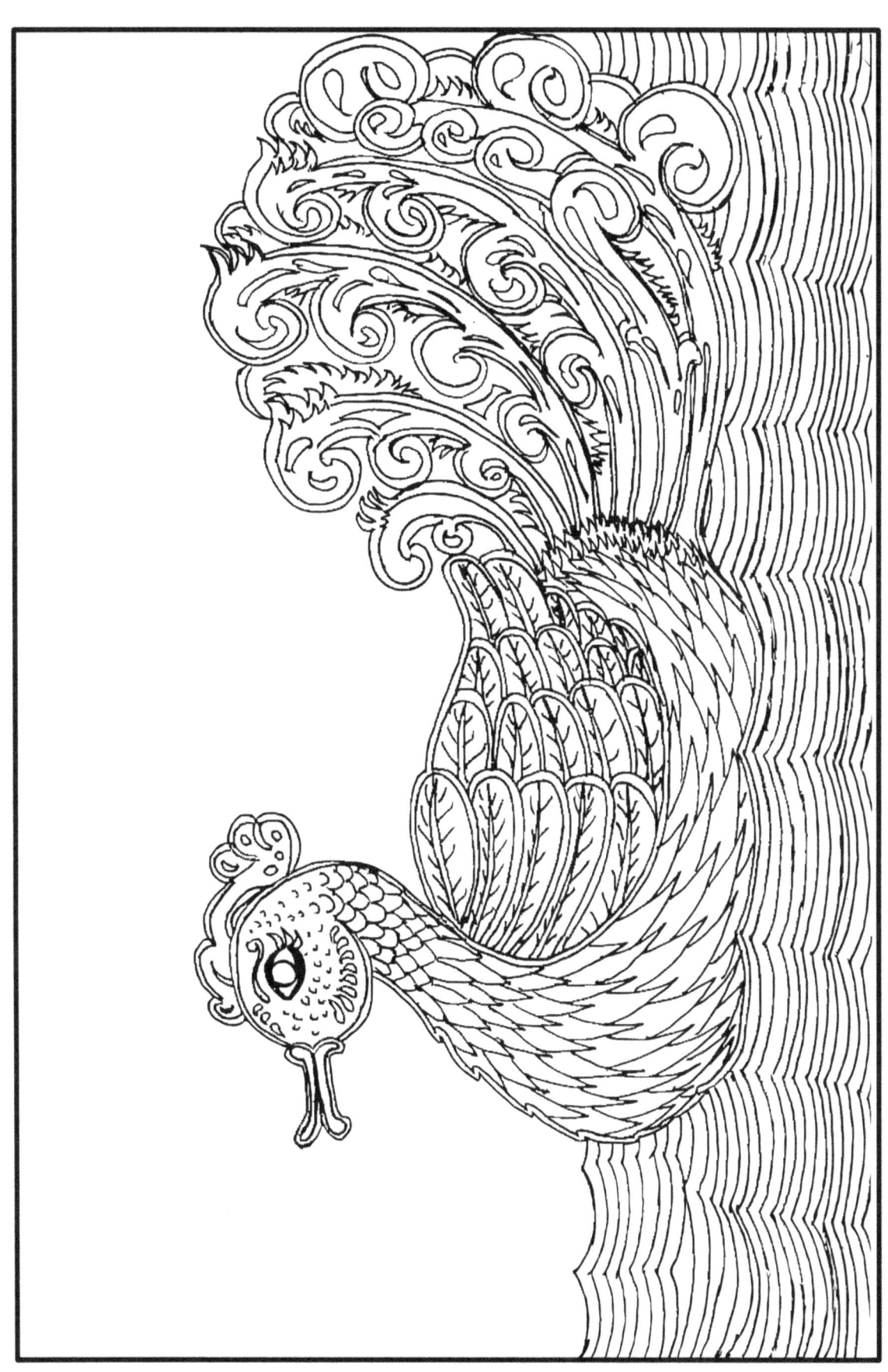

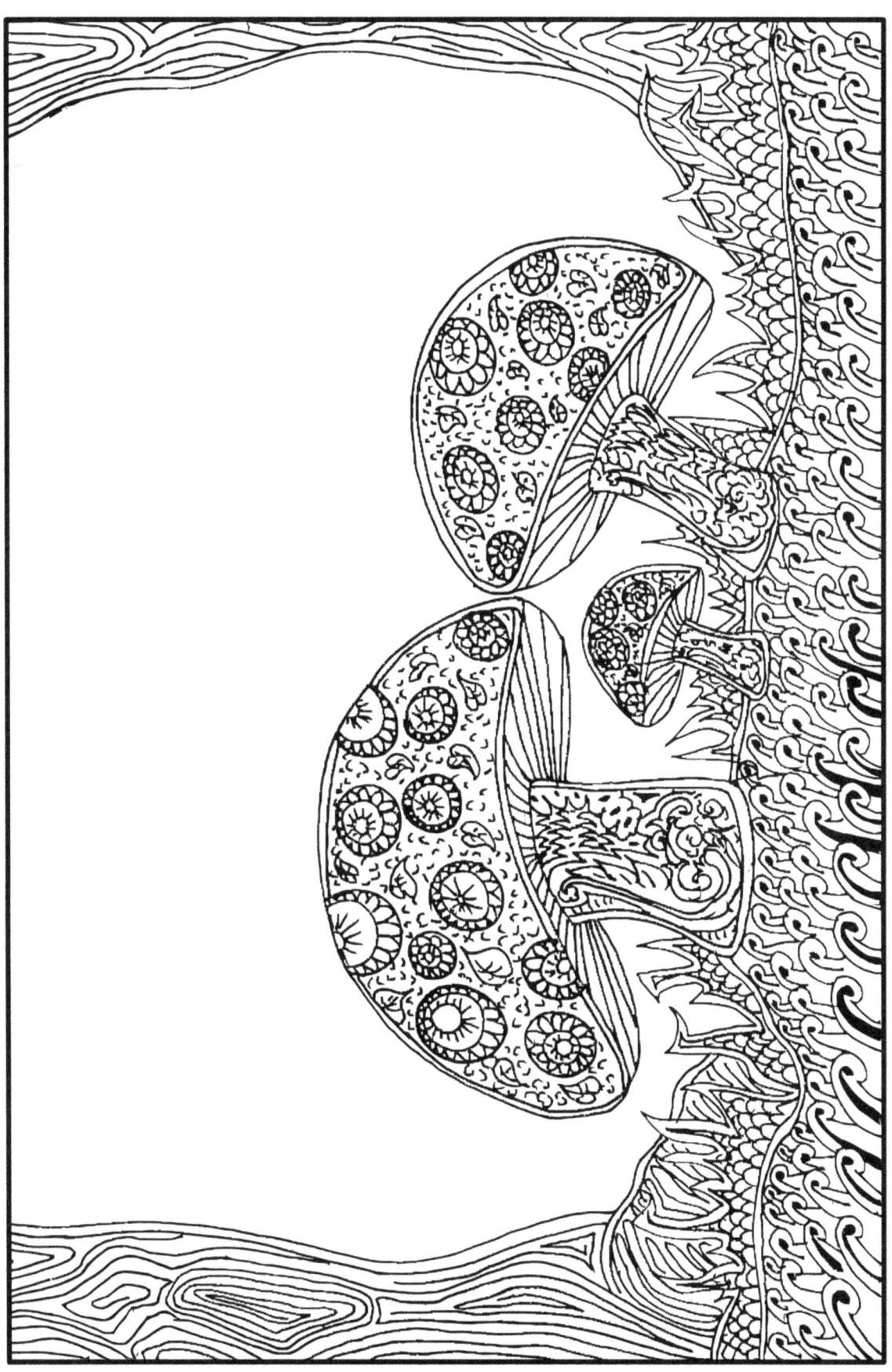

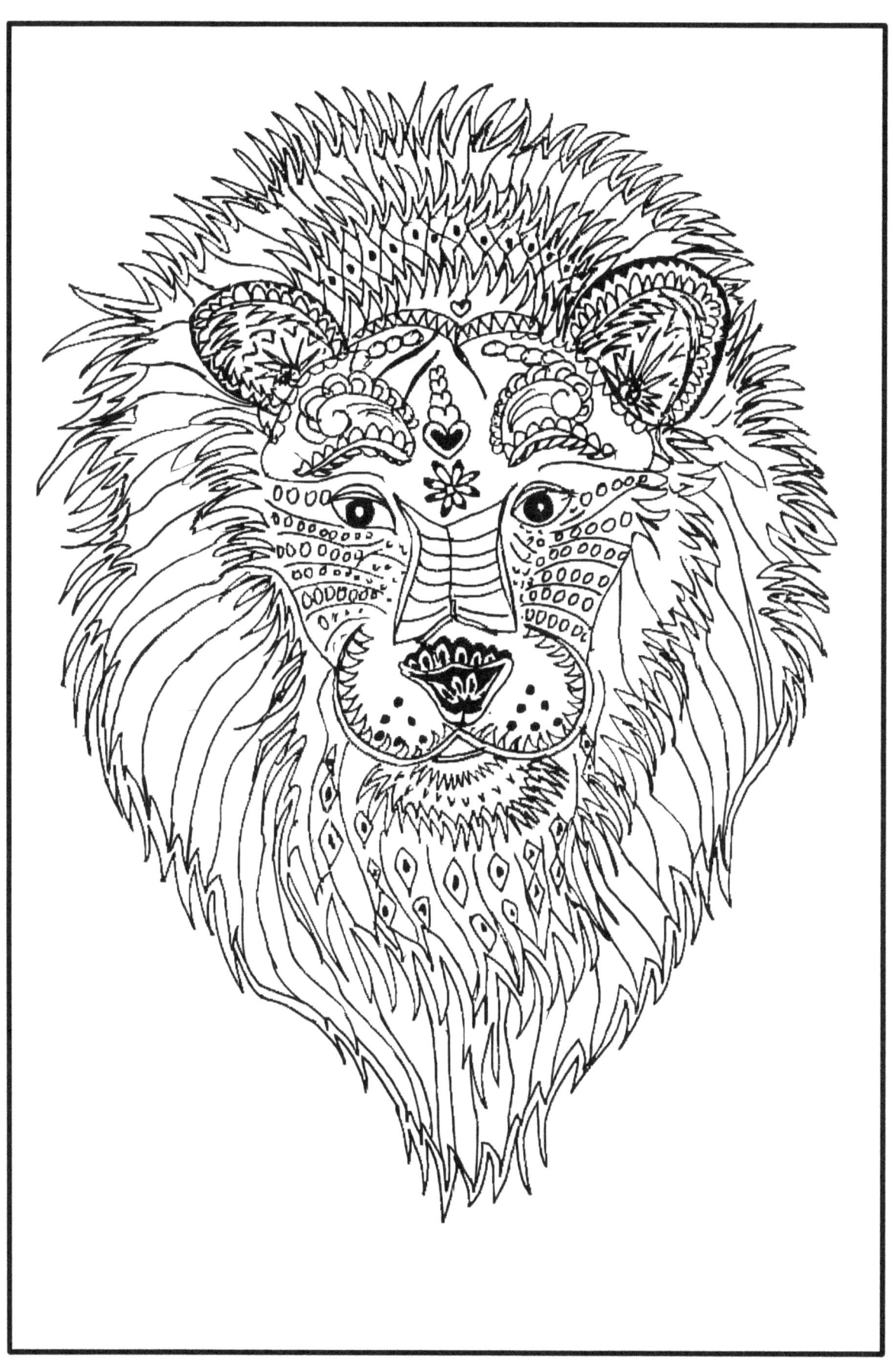

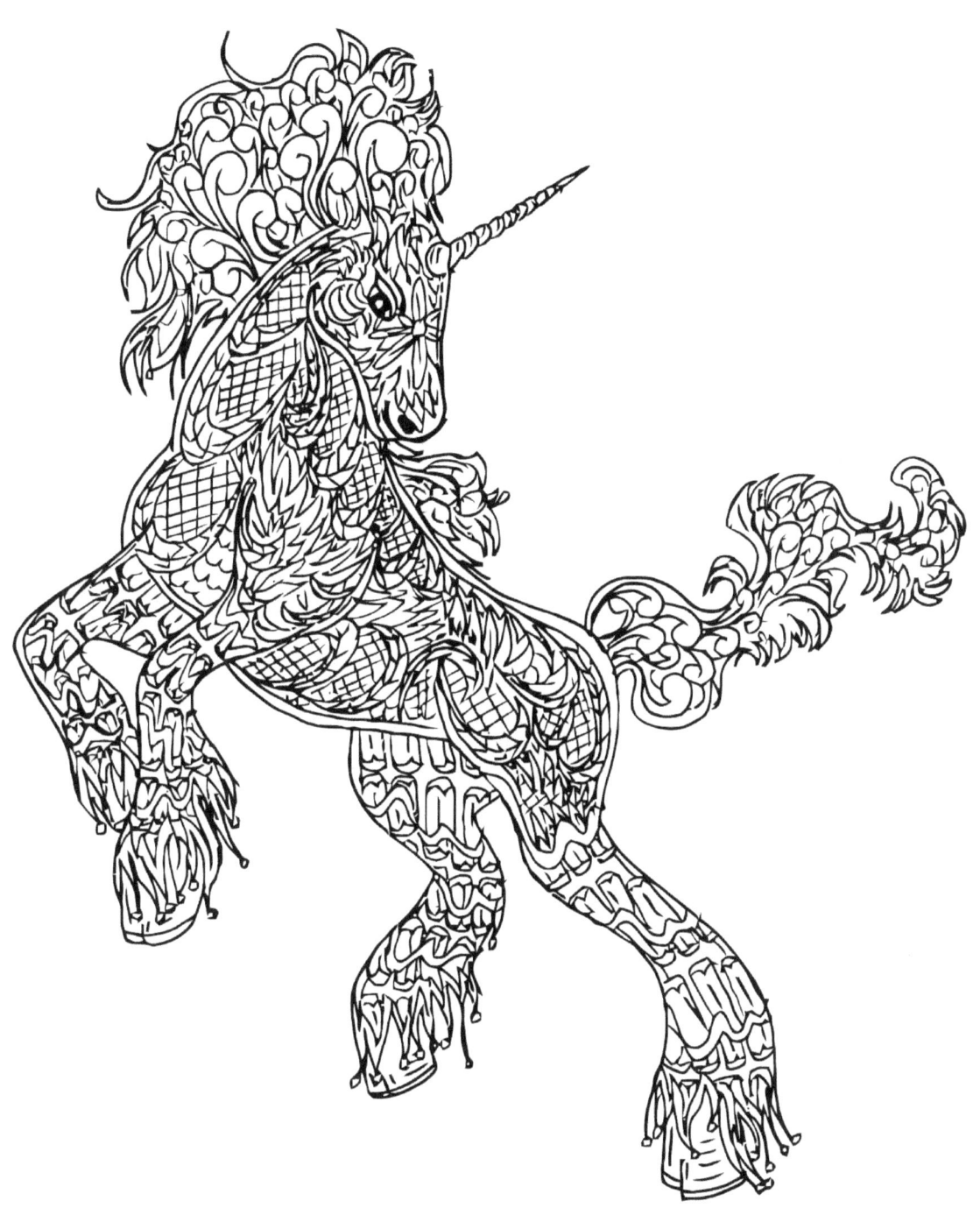

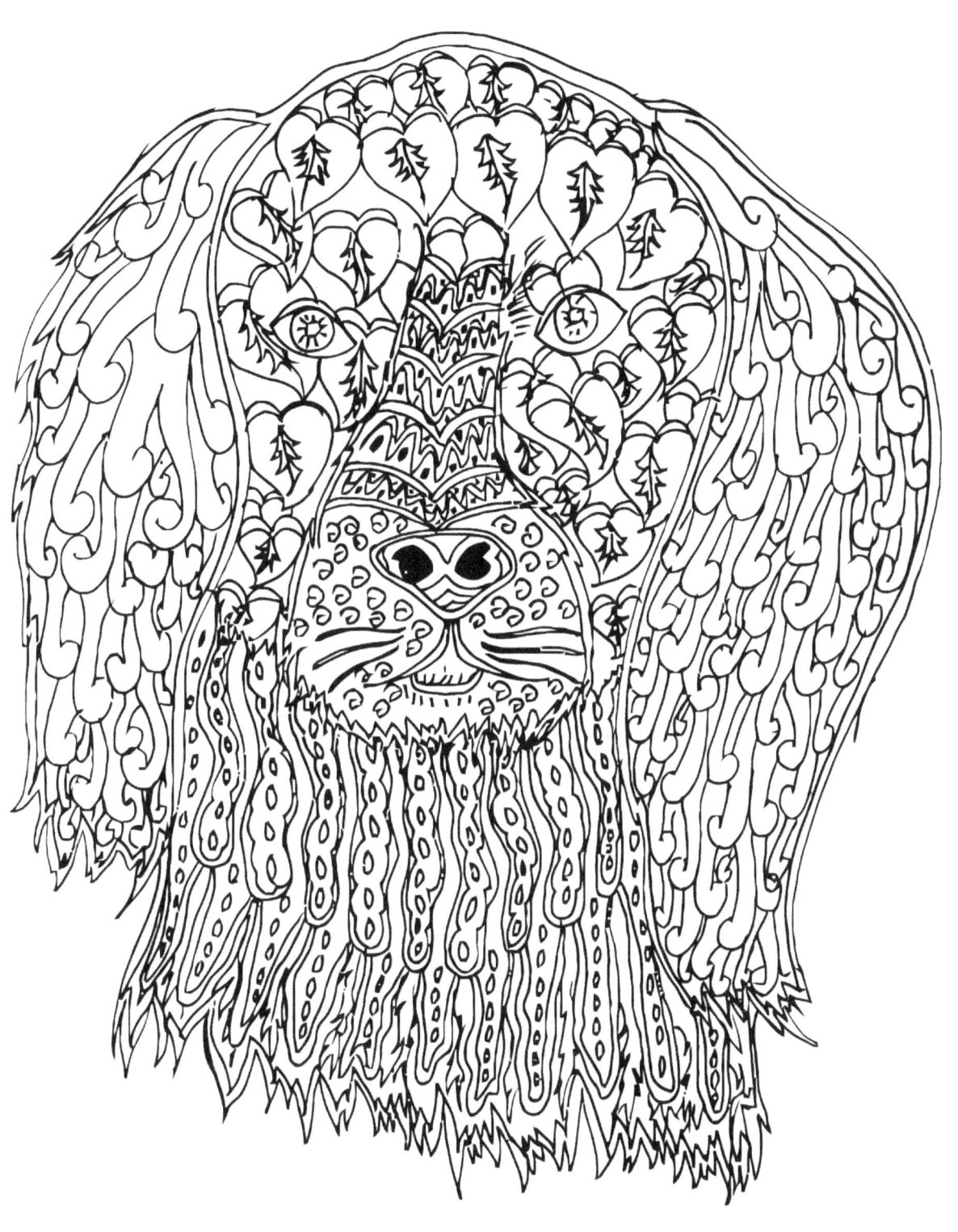

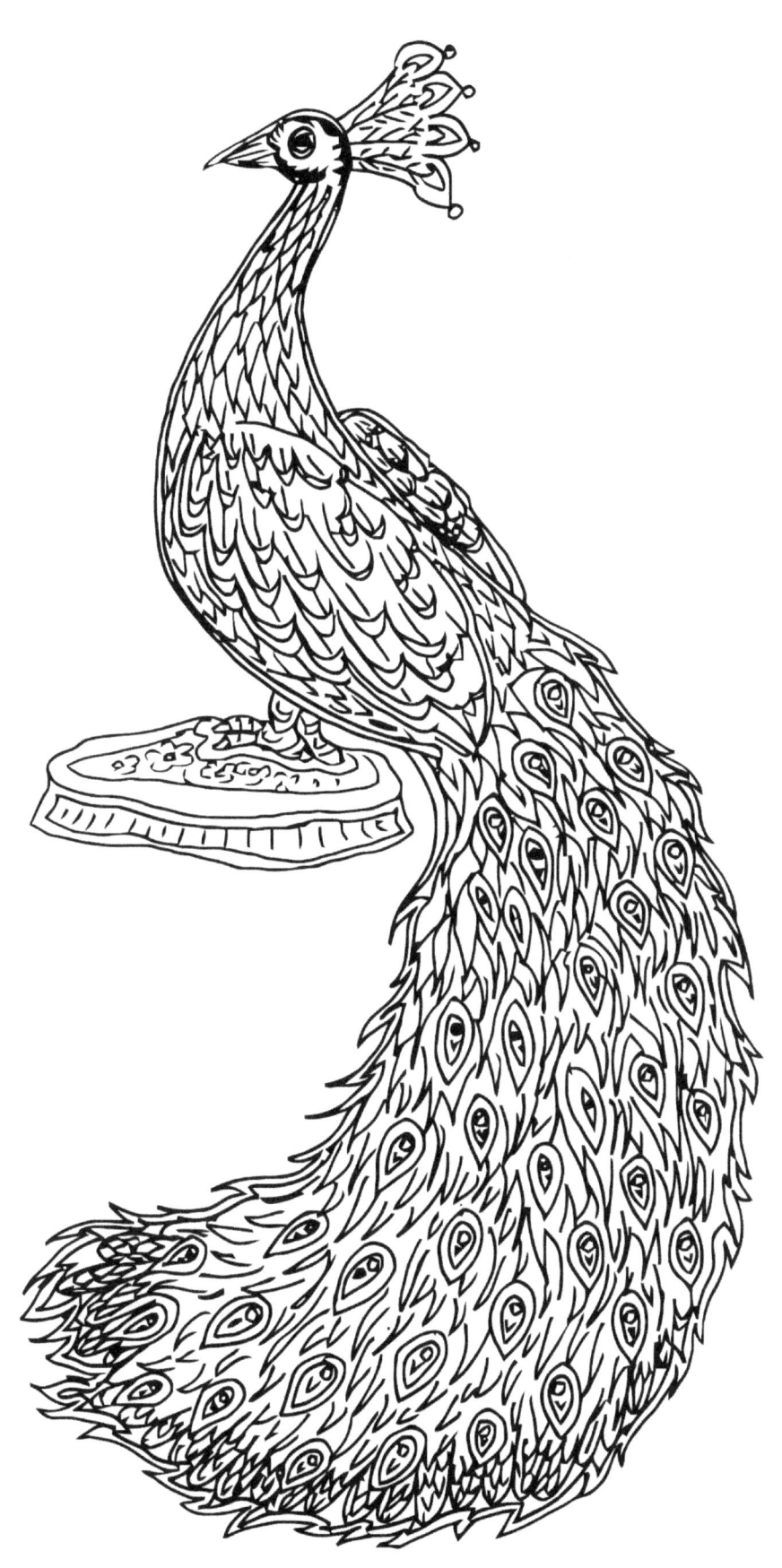

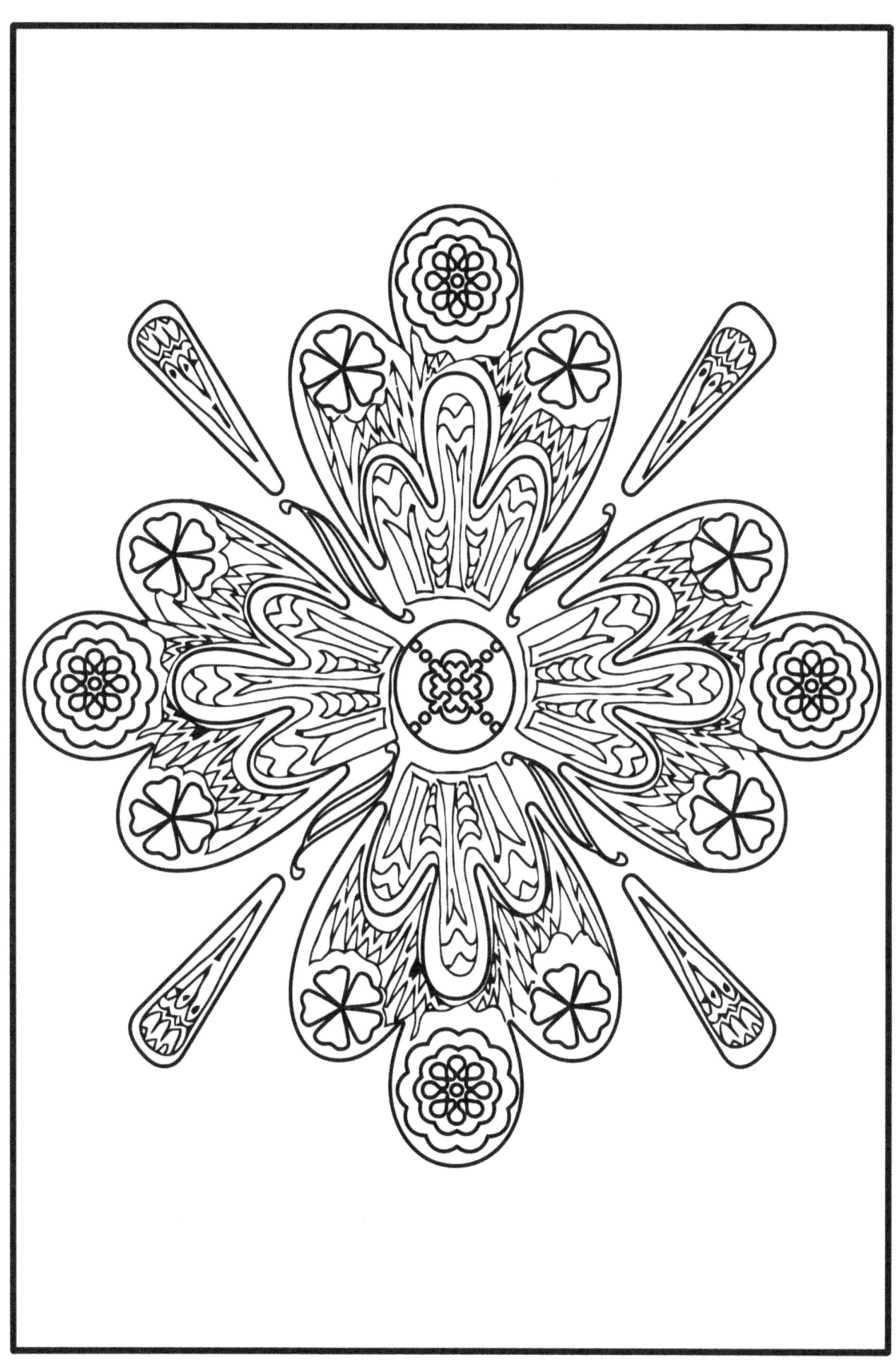

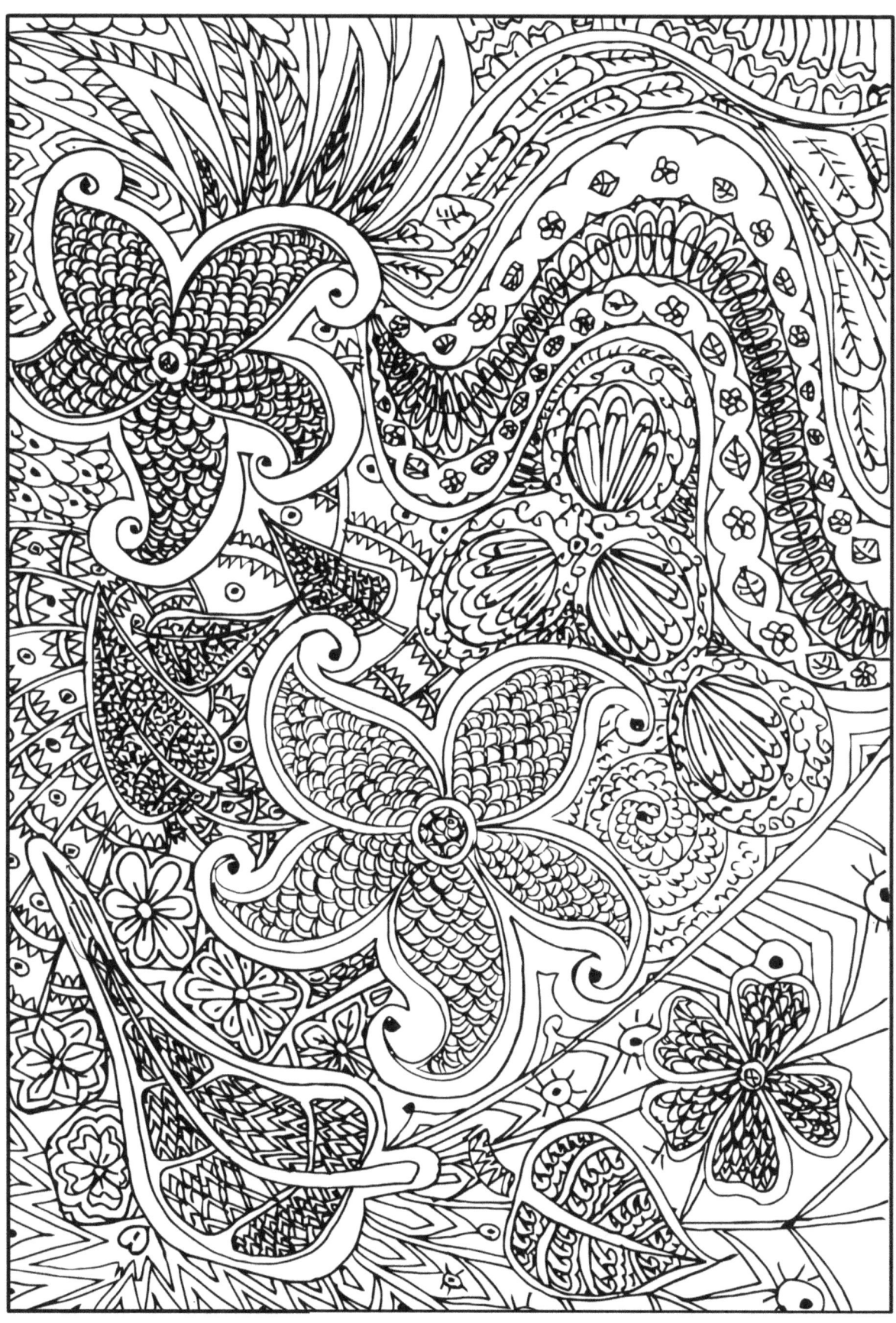

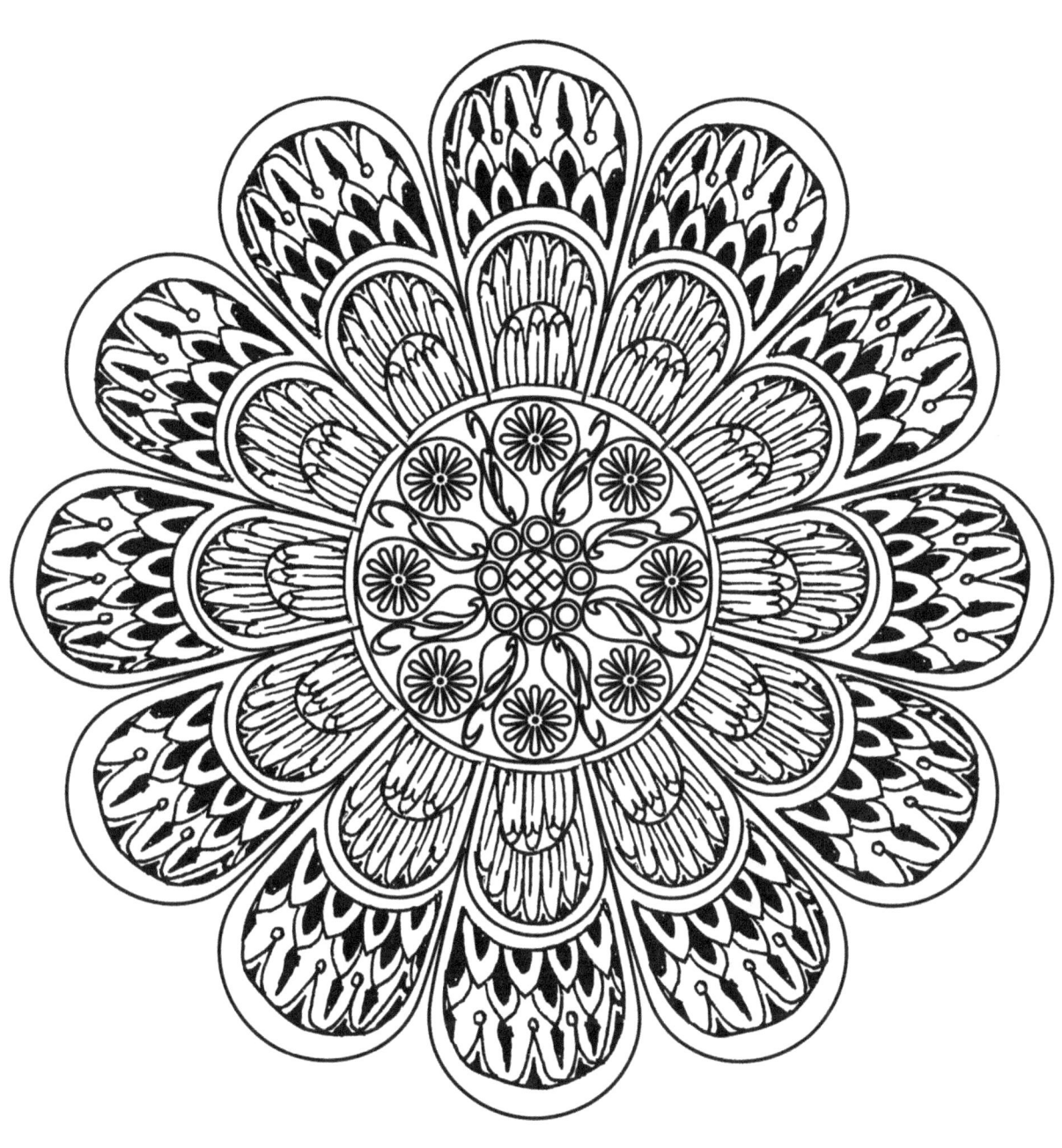

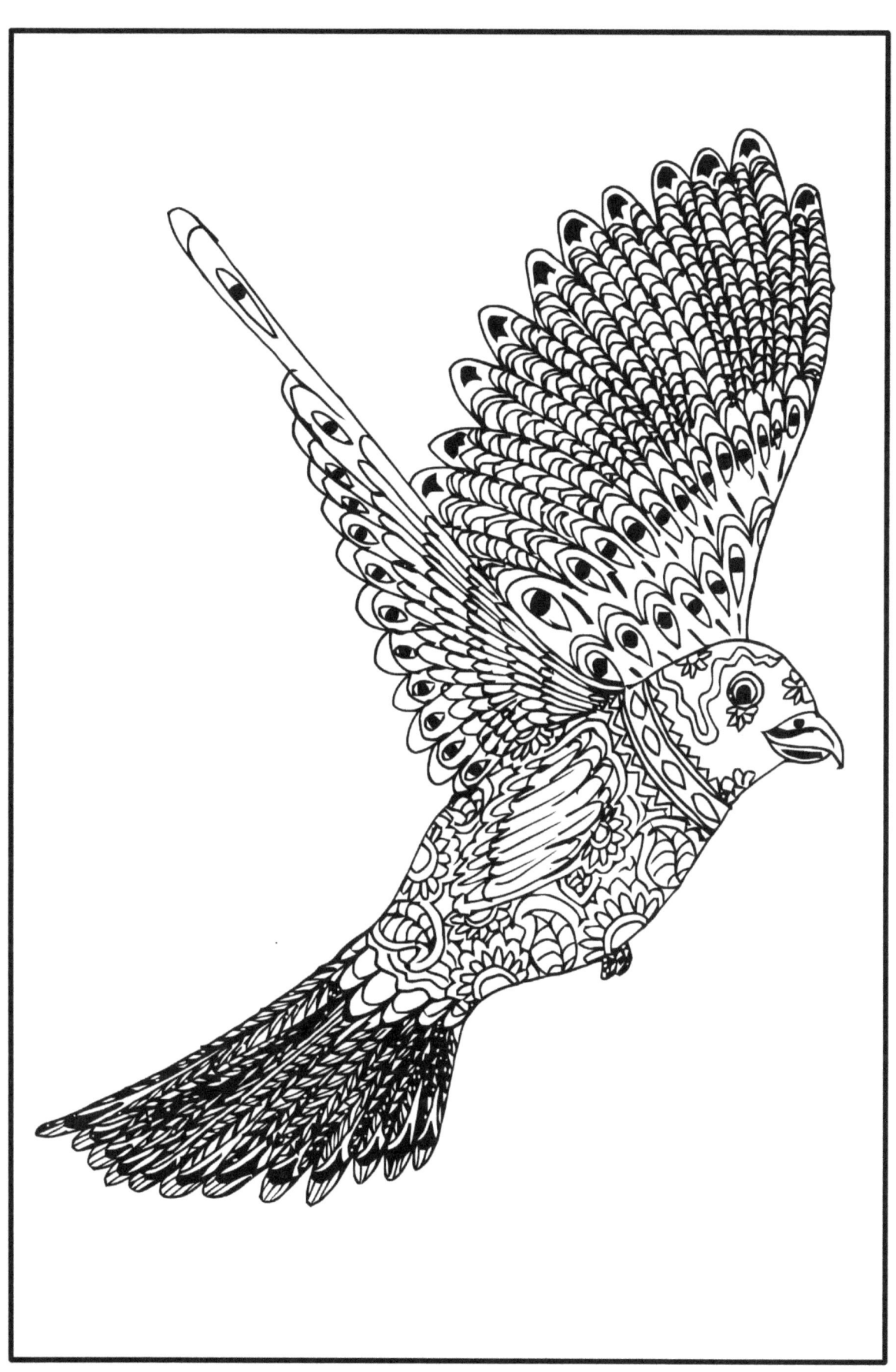

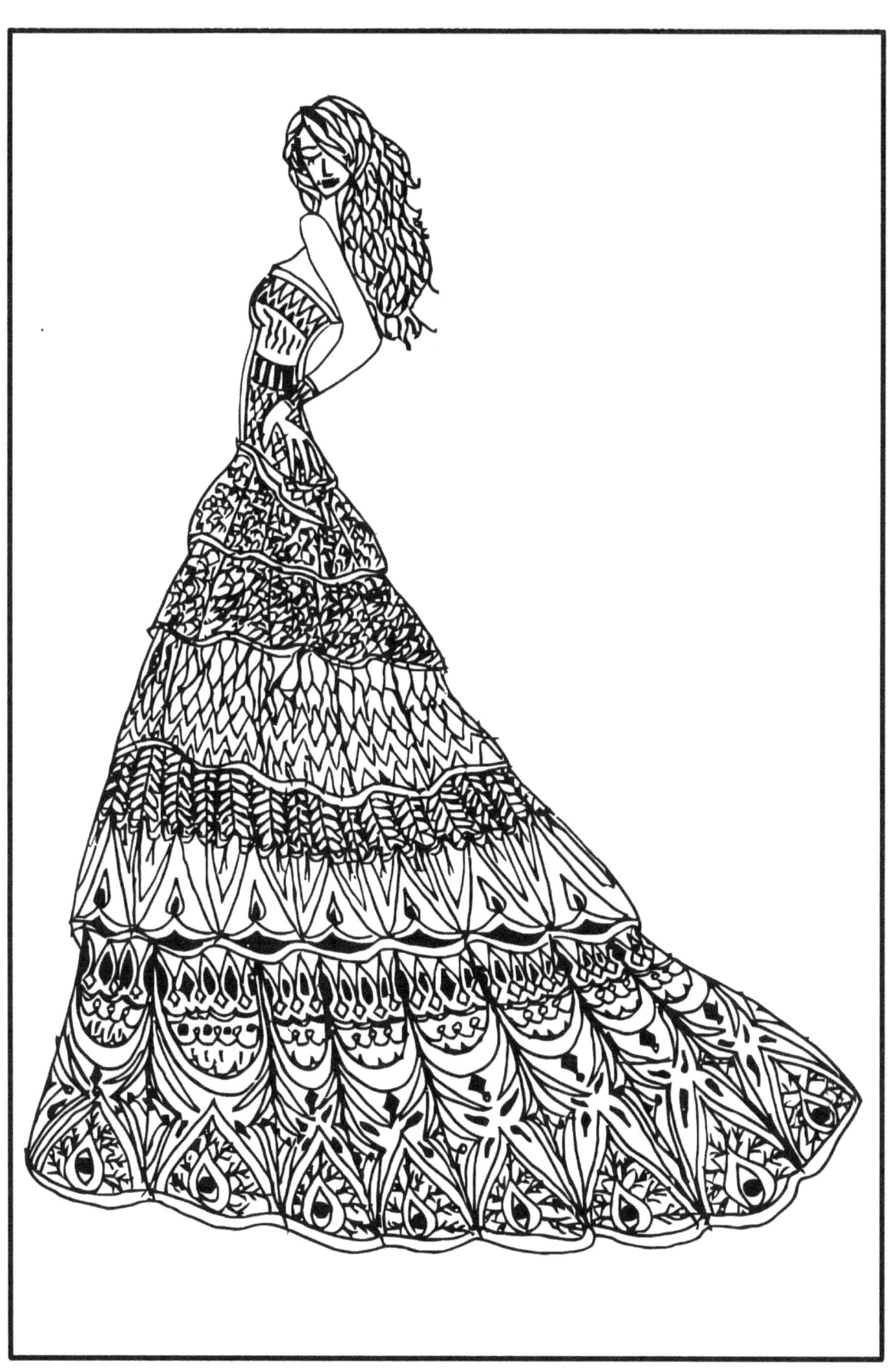

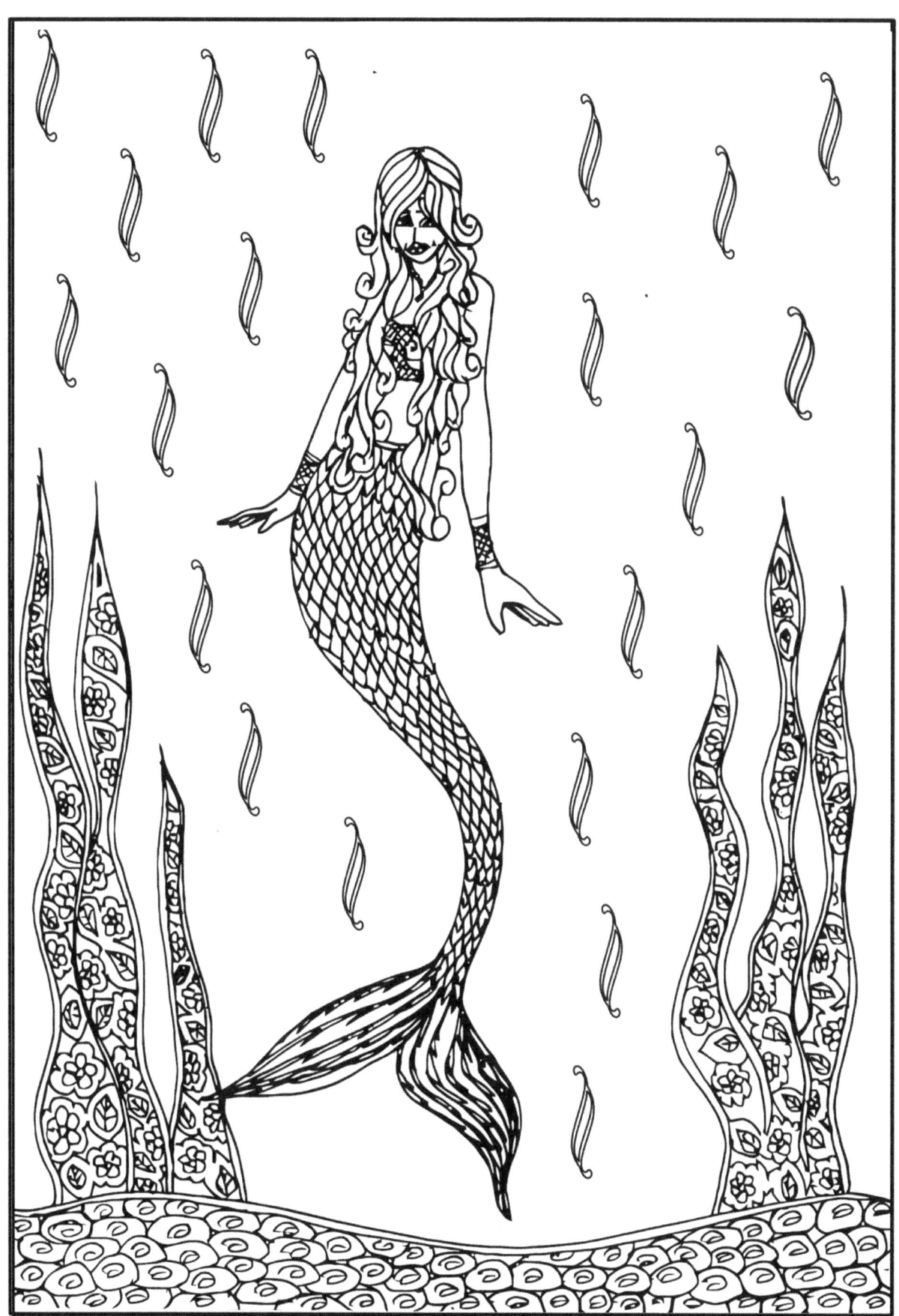

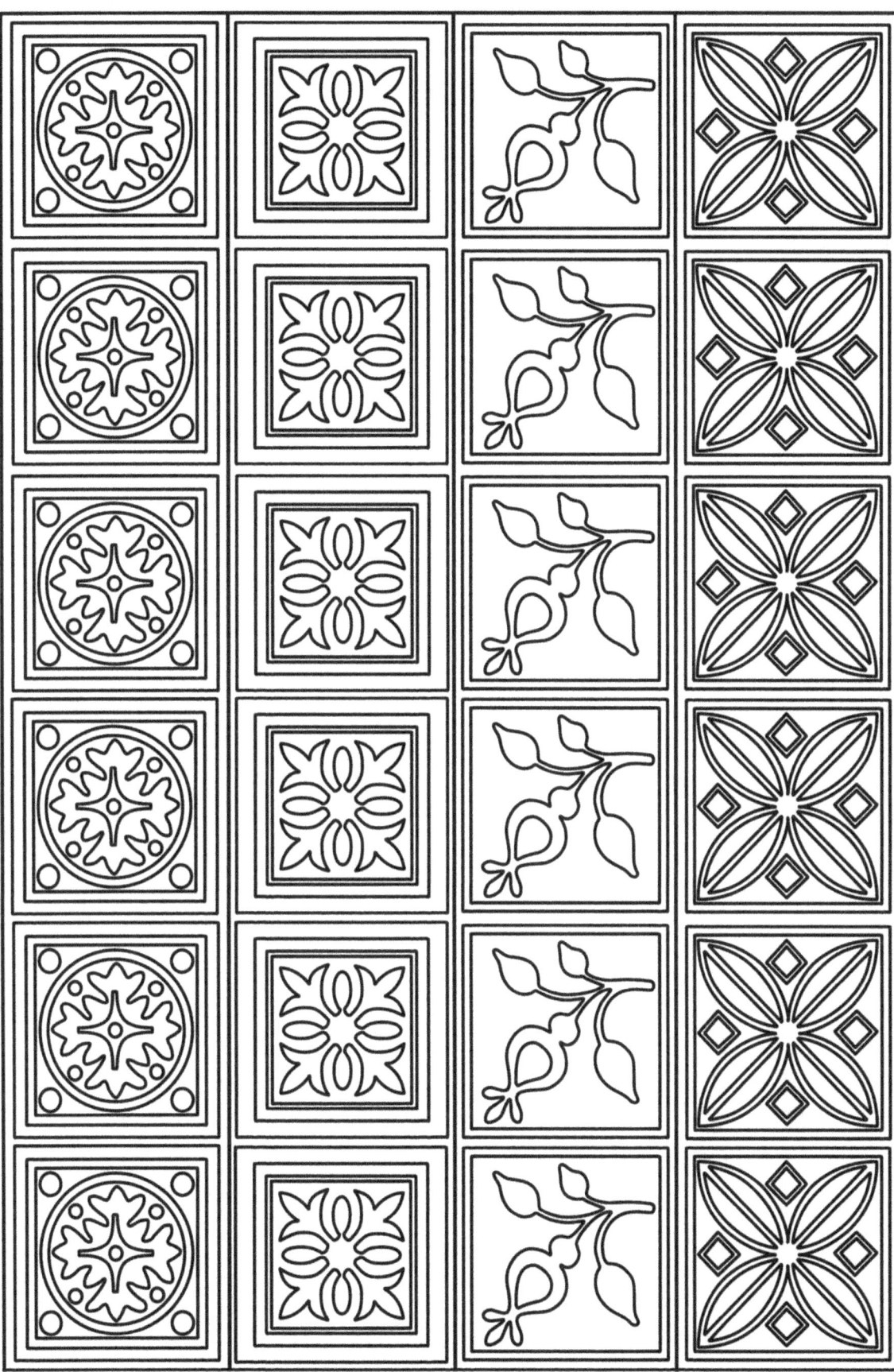

Be one of the In Crowd!

As a Mix Books Coloring Insider, you will receive FREE coloring pages to download and be among the first to know about give-aways, special offers, and our newest coloring books.

Sign up now, and as our thanks to you, immediately receive TEN illustrations in PDF format. Go to:

http://www.mix-booksonline.com/coloring

Look for other great coloring books from

mix-booksonline.com/category/coloring-books:

Paisley and Patterns: Intricate Designs Coloring Book

Stress Relief Coloring Book: Patterns & Designs

Adult Coloring Book for Relaxation: **SERENITY**

Adult Coloring Book: **Christmas Mandalas and Messages**

Coloring Book for Adults: **BadASS Buttocks**

FLOWERS: A Floral Inspiration Coloring Book

Coloring Book of Vintage Caricatures and Characters

Silesian Folk Tales Coloring Book: Intricate Vintage Illustrations

Fun, Fantasy and Fairy Tales: A Kid's Coloring Book

www.ingramcontent.com/pod-product-compliance
Lightning Source LLC
Chambersburg PA
CBHW082303200526
45168CB00017B/2757